The Household and the War for the Cosmos

THE HOUSEHOLD AND THE WAR FOR THE COSMOS

Recovering a Christian Vision for the Family

C. R. WILEY

Published by Canon Press
P.O. Box 8729, Moscow, Idaho 83843
800.488.2034 | www.canonpress.com

C.R. Wiley, *The Household and the War for the Cosmos: Recovering a Christian Vision for the Family*

Cover design by James Engerbretson
Interior design by James Engerbretson and Valerie Anne Bost

Printed in the United States of America.

Library of Congress Cataloging-in-Publication Data

Wiley, Chris, author.
The household and the war for the cosmos : Christian piety and the end of the world / by C.R. Wiley.
Moscow, Idaho : Canon Press, 2019
LCCN 2019011380 | ISBN 9781947644915 (pbk. : alk. paper)
LCSH: Families--Religious life. | Families--Religious aspects--Christianity. | Piety.
Classification: LCC BV4526.3 .W53 2019 | DDC 261.8/3585--dc23
LC record available at https://lccn.loc.gov/2019011380

19 20 21 22 23 24 24 9 8 7 6 5 4 3

For Marla,

For her worth is far above jewels

CONTENTS

FOREWORD

By Nancy Pearcey

WHEN I WAS YOUNGER, I WAS ATTRACTED to feminism. I scoured the shelves of the local library for feminist books, and always had one or two on my night stand. I read all the feminist classics and thought each was better than the one before.

My flirtation with feminism continued even after I married and gave birth to my first child. *Especially* after I had a child. At the time, I was attending seminary, and having a baby meant having to drop out of school. It seemed that I faced the bleak possibility of never fulfilling my deepest interests and calling. It struck me as decidedly unfair that men, when they become fathers, do *not* have to face the threat of losing their access to education and a vocation.

That made me wonder, Why do the paths for men and women diverge so sharply when they have children? As I researched the subject, I discovered that it was not always so. Before the industrial revolution, when economic work was performed within the household, both men and women spent most of their time in the home and its outbuildings. Fathers were able to be far more involved in childrearing than today. And mothers were able to be involved in economically productive work without putting the kids in day care.

Work was not the *father's job*, it was the *family industry*. Often the living quarters were in one part of the house, with offices, workshops, or stores in another part of the same house. Husband and wife worked side by side, not necessarily at identical tasks but sharing in a common economic enterprise.

That struck me as a much more balanced arrangement. How did we lose this vision of an integrated household?

The change started with the industrial revolution, which took work out of the home. The household was no longer the center of economic activity. Fathers had no choice but to follow their work out of the household and into factories and offices. As a result, they were simply not present at home enough to continue the same level of involvement in teaching and disciplining their children.

As for women, when household industries were transferred to the new factories, mothers at home were reduced from producers to consumers. Eventually not only economic production but also a host of social functions were moved out of the home—education was removed to schools; care of the sick and elderly was transferred to institutions; grandparents and singles moved out into separate homes and apartments; recreation became something you buy at the movie theater or engage in alone on your private electronics. Even family devotions were given up and parents came to rely on churches and youth groups. What remained in the home was little more than housework and early childcare.

No wonder feminists sensed that many of the rewarding and interesting activities of life had been transferred to the public realm!

When I discovered the negative effects caused by the break-up of the household, it made sense why the first wave of feminism emerged shortly after the industrial revolution. (I described this history in chapter 12 of my book *Total Truth.*) But feminism has not provided a solution. Just the opposite: It has urged women to strip the home still further by working outside and putting the kids in hired day care. Feminists have pushed for abortion and state-funded day care so women can prioritize work outside the home.

Sociologists tried to rationalize the breakdown of household as a good thing. They claimed that as the family lost its multiple functions—economic, educational, religious, medical—it would actually grow stronger. Why? Because, they said, the family would now be freed up to focus on its core function: emotional bonding.

But it is unrealistic to think that a group of people who have nothing in common will sit down together and relate emotionally to one another over nothing at all. And the fact is, they don't: Today family meals are rare. It has become difficult to sustain any family coherence as individuals disperse to their separate activities or become absorbed in their personal electronics. The rising rates of divorce, desertion, cohabitation, and single-parent homes makes it obvious that sheer emotional intensity is not enough to hold families together. Getting married and having children has been reduced to a lifestyle choice.

In fact, modern societies are rejecting even the biological basis of the family. When the U.S. Supreme Court legalized homosexual marriage, it did so on the grounds that sheer intensity of emotion between two people of any sex is enough to replace the biological correspondence between husband and wife.

Today the true revolutionaries are not feminists, homosexual activists, or other progressives but those who are seeking to halt any further erosion of the family, and even reverse the process—families who are intentionally working to restore at least some of the traditional functions of the household. Most obvious are homeschooling families who are bringing education back into the home. Then there are parents who are starting home-based businesses and family enterprises so that husband and wife can once again work together, while training their children in the skills needed for the workplace. (Advances in technology are making it easier for parents to bring work back into the home through things like telecommuting.) There are families who play games and read together instead of dispersing to their personal electronics. There are families who are restoring family devotions.

With such a rich and rewarding vision of the household, who *wouldn't* be inspired to invest in family life?

It is this vision of the restored household that Christopher Wiley wishes to impart to you as you read this book. He shows that having a family is not just a private, personal choice. Historically, the household has been the basis for the formation of all the other social institutions—school, church, business enterprise, city, nation. As the household goes, so go all the other institutions of society.

Recovering a vision for the household is no easy task. As Wiley writes, "Most books on marriage today, even those published by Christian authors, never get close to the household economy as it was practiced throughout the ancient world, and as it was described in the Bible." There is a reason the New Testament Christians greeted one another as brothers and sisters of the one Father God. There is a reason the relationship between the Christ and the Church is symbolized as a marriage. There is a reason

Paul addressed the Church as "members of the household of God" (Eph. 2:19). It is by living in a household, with its interconnected duties and dependencies, that we are trained in the ways the Church is meant to operate.

As we lose the very concept of the household, we are losing the "school" that trains us how to function with love and responsibility *beyond* the household.

Even specific verses in the Bible cannot be understood without knowing something about the pre-industrial household. Consider the passage telling fathers to bring up their children "in the nurture and admonition of the Lord" (Eph. 6:4, KJV). It is difficult for the modern office worker or factory worker who is gone from home all day to be their children's teacher in the way the Bible writers had in mind. They were thinking of fathers who spent the entire day with their wives and children—the kind of childhood Jesus would have experienced, working daily with his father in a carpenter's shop. We need to think carefully how much we have let our lives be captive to modern history and economic structures.

Or consider the passage urging women to be "workers at home" (Titus 2:5, NASB). Of course, at the time everyone was a worker at home—they worked on the farm or in a home industry or home-based craft. There was nowhere else to work! With a few exceptions like sailors and soldiers, men were workers at home as well. Even professional men, like lawyers and businessmen, worked in a home office. A proper understanding of the household may change the way we typically interpret this verse.

In this book, Christopher Wiley urges readers to take on "the recovery of the productive household." You don't have to agree with everything he writes to find that he paints a more inspiring view of the Christian life than we get from most sermons or devotional literature. In the ancient world, including the world of the Bible, people thought they lived in a natural order, and the household was part of that natural order. They did not think family relationships had to be invented from scratch or held together by sheer emotional intensity. Nor was the household limited to the stripped-down nuclear family. Extended family members and single people were also part of households. (Singles did not come home at night to a dark, empty apartment.) It was virtually impossible for anyone to survive outside a household, since that's where economic work took place. There was room for everyone within the household.

In our own day, both family formation and fertility have plummeted. The common wisdom is that the decline of the household was caused by the process of secularization. But in her book *How the West Really Lost God*, Mary Eberstadt argues that historically things happened the other way around: At least some of the time, the record suggests, people became secular *because* they stopped getting married and having children. When we grow up in broken and disordered families, we have no experience to understand the ordered structure of the household of God—or even the structure of the cosmos, which it reflects.

The structure of the cosmos? Yes, that's the larger point that Wiley argues in his expansive vision of family and Church. I invite you to enter into that vision. Wiley writes in an accessible yet illuminating style. You will be inspired, as I was, to a richer, fuller view of the family and its place in the order of reality.

PREFACE

By Anthony Esolen

MAN IS HARD OF HEART AND DOES NOT easily forgive. If only his mind were as tenacious as that. But he finds it easy to forget. It is often to his immediate advantage to do so, because it relieves him of many a heavy duty. So goes that sad song of Shakespeare's:

> Freeze, freeze, thou bitter sky
> That dost not bite so nigh
> As benefits forgot.*

Christopher Wiley is calling upon us to remember that we have duties that go by the name of *piety*, what those

* *As You Like It*, Act II, Scene 7.

duties are, why they have gone unregarded in our time, how they are founded in our human and bodily nature, and why they are essential for the Christian to practice. He does so in a way that engages the reader regardless of his education, but that is also informed by the best of ancient pagan wisdom, and the truth of the Scriptures. And he is cheerful about it, more cheerful by far than our obliviousness deserves.

This is not a Christian self-help book. Thank God for that. It is a call to wisdom and to action. "But my relationship to Jesus is personal," you may say, "and I don't see what it has to do with any other duties you might name." To be personal is already to be enmeshed in a web of responsibilities, in the duties of gratitude and love. Aeneas carried his crippled old father Anchises on his back, as Wiley shows us, not just because he had a peculiar love for the old man, but because *that is what the pious son must do.* If we lose this sense of filial piety, we might as well cease calling our God by the name Jesus teaches us to call Him: Father. And many a self-styled Christian has done so, Christians daring to imply that they are wiser than Jesus. At which point the faith staggers and falls, and what is left? A social club for old ladies with a taste for spirituality, no more significant than that; a beauty mark on the cheek of a dowager.

But God is our Father, "from whom all fatherhood in heaven and on earth is named," as Saint Paul says. God is the author of nature, and of our human nature, fallen though it may be through the sin of Adam. It makes no sense to think that we could ever understand the fatherhood of God without human fatherhood as its derivative and its image. Just as we cease to think of God as Creator, losing a strong sense of the ordered goodness of creation the more we ensconce ourselves in plastic and in the contra-natural habits of the sexual revolution, so the Father fades from our vision as patriarchy among us fades. The piety that God demands of us when He says, "Honour thy father and thy mother" (Exod. 20:12, KJV) is at one with the piety of the first commandment of all: "I am the LORD thy God . . . thou shalt have no other gods before me" (Exod. 20:2–3, KJV).

Piety tells us the truth about ourselves, too, in ways that contemporary man cannot easily recognize. "Honour thy father and mother," says Saint Paul, is "the first commandment with promise; that it may be well with thee, and thou mayest live long on the earth" (Eph. 6:2–3, KJV). That is fitting. Piety acknowledges the promise, in both directions of time. I am here and I am who I am because my father and mother, and their parents before them, made promises to one another, promises which they kept for one another and for their children. And I in turn have made the same promise to my wife, and that promise is made manifest in our own children and the care we have given to them. Man is not a flea in time. He dwells in a history, even that which goes back to Adam and extends to the end of time itself and its consummation in the heavenly

Jerusalem. Man dwells also in a place, a nation, and owes a debt of gratitude to all who came before him to give him what he, as an individual, can never repay. We are born the receivers of gifts: we are in debt from the start. Every breath we take is lent to us, and gratitude, pious gratitude, is the creature's share in the free abundance of the Creator.

What I've said here is just a part of what Christopher Wiley has said in this book, with all the verve of his manly spirit and the wealth of his experience as a husband, a father, a careful thinker about our social troubles, and a faithful Christian pastor. Read it, and remember that the one economy we are all called to join, the truest and most glorious economy, is that which cheers the pious psalmist's heart: "I was glad when they said to me, 'Let us go to the house of the LORD!'" (Ps. 122:1).

PART ONE
PIETY

1

THE DELUGE

THE SEED OF THIS BOOK WAS A TALK that I delivered in 2018 at the annual conference sponsored by Touchstone Magazine on the campus of Trinity University in Deerfield, Illinois. The conference included many excellent speakers, among whom were Nancy Pearcey and Anthony Esolen. I was honored to be included.

It was Nancy who encouraged me to begin this book by repeating some of the remarks I made when I introduced my talk. Those remarks were intended to help my listeners understand the reason for my interest in the things I write about, and on that day, spoke about.

My interest in households arises from the fact that I never really lived in one until I built one together with my wife. My earliest memories of home are full of tension and sadness. My parents had folded in on themselves; this was the 1960s, when turning inward was encouraged. Things went from bad to worse for the family, and we were downwardly mobile. We moved from rented house to rented apartment, to smaller apartment. Piecing things together, I believe this was due to my father's interest in spirituality. He was a seeker, like the great herd at the time. Everyone was seeking, but few were finding. To our impoverishment my father finally found himself in the Church of Scientology.

In case you have not heard, it is very expensive to be a Scientologist. Soon my parents were broke, and their marriage broke soon after that. Then my father disappeared, and in her own way, my mother did too. By the time I was eleven years old I was pretty much on my own. I lived in a housing project and I had a short stint in foster care. My teenage years were bleak. My only consolations were drawing—I dreamed of becoming a comic-book artist—and my best friend. My friend was a pastor's son. It was through his friendship that I eventually became a friend and follower of Christ.

When it was time for me to become a husband and eventually a father, I thought I should read up on those subjects, seeing as I had had little in the way of day-to-day experience witnessing a man performing those roles. Well, I am sorry to say that I didn't find much worth reading in the Christian bookstores that I visited. Most of the stuff was pop-psychology with a Jesus gloss.

I wanted to get down to the roots of things. That's how I came to read people like Allan C. Carlson, Christopher Lasch, and Robert Nisbet. But even more helpful have been Aristotle, Xenophon, and Virgil, as you will soon see.

Of course, above them all stands the Bible. Once you know what a household looks like you can see that the Bible is a kind of handbook for households.

THE LEVEE IS BROKEN

I'm not the only person in the world to come from a broken home. The experience is so common these days you could almost say that it is the norm. What started as a crack in the levee of social standards has become a wide breech, and a torrent of chaos has poured through. Our civilization is washing away. Although my parents were too old to be hippies in the 60s, they felt the early effects of the turn away from norms that had seemed so solid right into the 1950s. That solidity was an illusion. We know that now. The foundation of those norms was already deeply compromised by the time I was born.

In the part of Connecticut where I live today we literally have crumbling foundations everywhere. The reason is a mineral that went undetected in a concrete mix from a local quarry. For years this quarry churned out the bad mix and no one knew—not even the owners of the quarry.

In some cases million-dollar homes that look fine from the street stand condemned.

Metaphorically, something similar has occurred in our culture. Western civilization still has curb appeal. Things like economic growth, advances in medicine, and an emphasis on human rights seem to indicate that things are in good shape. But something has been added to the mix that serves as the intellectual and spiritual basis for our society. The institutions at the foundation of our way of life don't seem solid any longer. And the most important of these institutions is the household.

Paradoxically, many of the other institutions in our society that once relied upon the household have turned against it. Everything from multi-national corporations to public schools now dismiss traditional household norms as retrograde and even oppressive. And I am sorry to say that even evangelical Christianity increasingly looks like a fair-weather friend.

Just in case you're tempted to write this off as alarmist, consider the following:

1. Marriage has been reduced to a lifestyle choice.

I can remember when politicians called traditional marriage the "foundation of our society." Hardly anyone calls it that today. Instead marriage is a matter of taste. And apparently fewer people have a taste for it these days, if the numbers can be trusted. Across the world the average age of a person getting married continues to go up even as the percentage of people getting married goes down. Mark Regnerus, a sociologist at the University of Texas, documents some startling data. Consider this: in 1980 91% of Czech women were married by the time they were 30 years old. Today it is 26%. And it is the same everywhere. In 1980 81% of Australian women were married by 30 years of age, in Finland, 66% of women, in Italy, 76% of women, and in the Netherlands, 81% of women. Today the numbers are between 20% and 30% in each of those countries.

People are also experimenting with marriage. There's so-called "gay marriage"—but that's almost passé. There's polyamorous marriage, and open marriage, and marriage to vegetation (I heard of a woman that married a tree), and marriage to inanimate objects (I heard of another woman that married a bridge). I recently read of a woman who actually married *herself.* I could go on, but that would be tedious.

Many churches are eager to bless all of this. Since God loves us unconditionally, He (or She, once you start thinking this way) blesses everything. And even ostensibly conservative churches focus more on emotional satisfaction than on the functions that marriage once performed. If you don't know what I mean, pick up just about any book on marriage from an evangelical press.

2. Children are increasingly believed to be useless, or even bad to have.

Because we don't know what children are good for, we're having fewer of them. Fertility is plummeting across the world. This is greeted as something to celebrate by "humanitarians," except in places where they are finally feeling the effects of it. In Japan for instance the population declined by 449,000 in 2018. Even historically Roman Catholic countries cannot sustain their populations.

Besides, everyone knows that kids are expensive; in 2017 the US Department of Agriculture estimated that it will cost $233,610 to raise a child to 17 years of age. Not only that, children can hurt your feelings. Dogs are less expensive, and they're always happy when you come home.

But even when people manage to have children they treat them like pets, things to lavish ourselves upon, but not depend upon. And like a self-fulfilling prophecy, when these children reach adulthood, often you can't depend upon them.

3. Post-familialism is on the rise.

Since marriage and children are believed to be more trouble than they're worth, more and more people are just opting out of family life. Something has emerged that once would have been considered an absurdity—the single person household.

I see it especially with middle-aged women that work for large corporations. Many of them are divorced.

Apparently their marriages weren't as emotionally gratifying as they thought they should be. And since many of them have exchanged a family for a career, their social needs are met at work.

Rather than challenge this, or even question it, many evangelicals, especially in coastal cities, justify it, citing 1 Corinthians 7 and Paul's reflections on the advantages that he enjoyed as an unmarried apostle. Oddly this is packaged with the Protestant doctrine of "the priesthood of all believers," so now celibacy is for everybody—not just the priesthood. (And as a bonus, this is marvelously helpful if your personal conceit is climbing the corporate ladder for Jesus.)

4. We're sliding into Socialism.

Concurrent with these things, and acting as both a cause and an effect, is the growth of the welfare state, and a push for Socialism.

It's an effect because many people don't have a family to fall back upon. And it's a cause because many people think that they don't need a family because they can always fall back upon the welfare state.

Naturally, this leads to childless people free-riding a system designed to work only so long as the population grows. In the long run the situation is unsustainable. When more and more people depend on a system that has fewer and fewer people pay into it, eventually things go bust.

5. **Finally, Christians are losing the ability to think like Christians.**

The language of our faith is largely drawn from the traditional household. God the Father, the only begotten Son, joint heirs with Christ, a bride adorned for her husband, the marriage supper of the Lamb—all of these things tell us what the faith is, and how to live it.

What is Christianity left with when we no longer live in households? I think that we are beginning to see it. If you're a political or social liberal, you're left with the de-gendered god of "social justice"; on the other hand, if you're just the typical consumer of religious goods, Jesus is now your personal "life-coach" and success guru. What you don't have in either case is a traditional household, or biblical Christianity.

So, what can we do about this? A great deal. And as you've probably guessed, that is what this book is for.

But I need to warn you, at first glance my approach may seem wildly impractical. What do I mean? First of all, I begin with the subject of piety, something so old-fashioned you may not have even have heard of it. And the second part of the book is given over to the subject of the cosmos, something that sounds so incredibly remote you probably can't even imagine how it could be relevant to your daily life.

But I promise, these things are not out-of-date or irrelevant. They're absolutely essential if we're going to recover the traditional household in our time. Please allow me to show you why.

2

WHATEVER BECAME OF PIETY?

WHY DON'T PEOPLE TALK ABOUT PIETY these days? In the circles where the word was once common currency it is kept locked up, perhaps waiting for the day it will be valued again, although I doubt that this is the intent. I suspect it has more to do with embarrassment, or perhaps puzzlement, like when you've come across some odd tool in your grandfather's garage and you have no idea what it is for.

I have a friend that collects old tools, manual drills and such. Some of them are quite exotic. When I'm at his place and I see them on the wall I make conversation by speculating on their former uses. To imagine what they were for, you have to enter a lost world, and sometimes my guesses make my friend smile. Other times he's just as puzzled by the tools as I am.

Piety is like that. For some people anything that seems old-fashioned is dismissed with an indifferent shrug. The more literate may sense its religious connotations. But just what it was good for is anyone's guess.

Providentially, as I was working on this chapter, I was sitting in the lobby of an automotive repair shop waiting for my Jeep to finish its emissions inspection. I was writing in a notebook and next to me sat an elderly woman. "What are you writing?" she asked. I looked up and forced a smile. "A book," I said, thinking that would be enough to allow me to go back to my writing. It wasn't. "Oh, about what?" she said, moving to the edge of her seat. "It's about piety," I replied, again thinking that this would be the end of it. If the subject of religion can't end a conversation, what can? I was wrong again. "What's piety?" she asked.

Think about this for a second. Here was a woman who looked to be in her seventies and she didn't know what piety is.

"It is something related to religion," I told her. At last, the conversation ended. Then the guy behind the desk said my Jeep was ready.

I am old enough to remember when preachers promoted piety—particularly those whose vocabulary had been formed by reading 18th century evangelists like John Wesley or George Whitfield. In the old days people believed in the meanings of words, and they stuck with them.

And if a person didn't understand a word, you defined it for them. And if he didn't like its meaning, you'd try to help him see the value of the word anyway. Imagine that.

I can recall when people changed their minds about the word *piety*. Younger men began to prefer younger sounding terms. The word *devotions* was popular. Later, more sophisticated people preferred the term *spiritual disciplines*. Publishers really ran with that for a while. But folksy youth pastor types liked *Quiet Time*, QT for short.

There has been something of a downgrade here, even with *spiritual disciplines*. Can you detect it? Words retain an aftertaste, even when the old meanings are lost. Originally, piety said something like a mode of life. QT is for your to-do list.

This reveals something about the state of religion in our time. Now, *religion* is another word that has fallen out of favor. The Latin root, *religio*, means to bind. Is it any wonder that the apostles to popular culture now insist that "Christianity is not a religion; it is a relationship"? You may have heard that slogan somewhere. But is it so? Does that do religion justice? The reason for bringing this up is what has happened to piety has also happened to religion. Both have been downgraded.

As wonderful as a personal relationship with Jesus is, the people that show the most enthusiasm for it do not give much thought to all the things that have to be in place in order for it to be possible. Take the Bible, for instance, or the sacraments, or the creeds, or even prayer. All of these things must be in place before you can even imagine having a personal relationship with Jesus. Without archivists, and translators, and publishers, we wouldn't have Bibles that tell us about Jesus. Then there are Church councils that gave us the creeds which summarize what the Bible says about Jesus and His divine nature. And this is just a start. Even beyond those things, just consider all the ways that the Christian religion has influenced Western civilization for the good. Think about how the arts, the sciences, and our laws, customs, and holidays wouldn't even exist in their current forms without the Christian religion. No, you cannot reduce Christianity to a relationship; it is bigger than that. *Religion* really is a better word than *relationship* for describing what it is.

And I believe that the same goes for piety.

EVERY WORD MATTERS

If you ask someone to define the word *synonym* the definition you get will probably be something like, "a word that can substitute for another word." But there really aren't any true synonyms in this sense. Each word has its own history, and subtle things about it that distinguish it from similar words. *Relationship* doesn't really substitute for *religion*, and *devotions* won't do as a substitute for piety. The drive to find substitutes for old-fashioned words unintentionally eliminates meanings. We can see how it works it in the book *1984*. There we have a fellow named Syme speaking to another fellow named Winston about the glories of "Newspeak" and their labors together at the Ministry of Truth:

> It's a beautiful thing, the Destruction of words. Of course the great wastage is in the verbs and adjectives, but there are hundreds of nouns that can be got rid of as well. It isn't only the synonyms; there are also the antonyms. After all, what justification is there for a word, which is simply the opposite of some other word? A word contains its opposite in itself. Take "good," for instance. If you have a word like "good," what need is there for a word like "bad"? "Ungood" will do just as well—better, because it's an exact opposite, which the other is not. Or again, if you want a stronger version of "good," what sense is there in having a whole string of vague useless words like "excellent" and "splendid" and all the rest of them? "Plusgood" covers the meaning or "doubleplusgood" if you want something stronger still. Of course we use those forms already, but in the final version of Newspeak there'll be nothing else. In the end the whole notion of goodness and badness will be covered by only six words—in reality, only one word. Don't you see the beauty of that, Winston? It was B.B.'s idea originally, of course," he added as an afterthought.*

* George Orwell, *1984* (1949; New York: Houghton Mifflin Harcourt, 2017), 49.

George Orwell, the author of *1984*, was quite concerned about thought control. "B.B." in the quotation above is a reference to Big Brother—the face of the political regime (note the nervous attribution of credit to him for the Destruction of words). Big Brother wants a compliant populace and removing troublesome words made that more likely. Orwell intuited a connection between words and meanings.* Eliminate a word and you eliminate an idea, and, by implication, a way of living that the idea suggests.

Let me give you an example of how this is done in real life. I lived and worked in Cambridge, Massachusetts, for nearly a decade. If you've heard of Cambridge, you have likely heard that it is a very liberal and progressive place. One day a woman in my church told me that she was no longer allowed to use the word *husband* in the public school that she worked for. She could only refer to him as her *partner*. What do you suppose was the reason for that? The authorities at her school wanted to prevent any sense that marriage should be limited to a union of a man and a woman. By the way, this happened back in the early 1990s. Trying to control thought by controlling language isn't as new as you may have supposed.

* Orwell's notion that ideas and words are inextricably linked is expressed in the word *logos*—a rich Greek word that has done a great deal to help us understand the world. *Logos* means both "word" and "reason," implying a linkage. It's the root of the English word *logic*, and the basis for the suffix affixed to the names of many academic disciplines, such as theology. The question Orwell doesn't address is the question, "Are our words the only words?" Both the Bible and Platonists would say "no."

While losing words is a big problem you don't actually need to *lose* a word to lose a meaning. You can obscure it by the subtle misuse of a word. And over time a new meaning can actually overshadow the original. It can even contradict it. You can see this with the word *freedom*, for example. Once it meant taking care of oneself. Now it means making other people support your choices.

When it comes to piety something along this line had already happened by the time the preachers of my youth commended it to me. I hate to say it, but even the piety of Wesley and Whitfield was a downgrade of the real thing.†

This is because by the eighteenth-century piety's sphere had already contracted. It is a well-documented story, so I won't go into detail, but I think I can sum it up succinctly. By the time of Wesley and Whitfield, what had once been regarded as public truth had been reduced to private convictions.

Authority in general had eroded due to revolutions in politics, the sciences, and even economics. To meet the challenge evangelists were forced to stress direct, very personal experience of the supernatural by everyone. The second-hand Truth contained in catechisms and confessions was no longer enough. Even eyewitness accounts of the risen Christ were not as trustworthy as a "warmed heart." This is how we ended up with a hymn like "I Serve a Risen

† See James D. Garrison, *Pietas from Vergil to Dryden* (University Park, PA: Pennsylvania State University Press, 1992), for the long, convoluted story of the transformation of the word piety into what we know today.

Savior." In that song the line that is supposed to persuade you to believe that Jesus rose from the dead is, "You ask me how I know He lives? He lives within my heart!"*

What we are left with today is heart religion, because now the heart is the only place Jesus can be publicly acknowledged to live. Ironically, many people think that this is the sum total of Christianity, and the notion that this is actually a downgrading of the faith is inconceivable.

WHAT DOES HEART RELIGION LOOK LIKE?

Allow me to use an image to show you. When it comes to heart-religion, the image that comes to mind for me is found in the old song "In the Garden."

Now I know the song well. When I was a pastor on Cape Cod, I sang it a lot. Cape Cod is one of those places that people go to die, like Florida. So I buried a lot of folks during my time there. Following a death, I would meet with the family in order to plan the funeral. We'd discuss eulogies, Scriptures to read, and of course, songs to sing. And "In the Garden" was second only to "Amazing Grace" when it came to most requested hymns.

Here's the first verse, in case you've never heard it.

> I come to the garden alone,
> While the dew is still on the roses.
> And the voice I hear, falling on my ear
> The Son of God discloses—

* Alfred H. Ackley, © 1933. Renewed 1961 Word Music, LLC.

There are two more verses like it, but I'll spare you. Besides, it is the refrain that really sticks with you. Here's how that goes:

> And He walks with me, And He talks with me.
> And He tells me I am His own.
> And the joy we share, as we tarry there,
> None other has ever known.†

"None other has ever known." What's that supposed to mean? Everything, I believe. And that's the trouble.

"In the Garden" was immensely popular back in the day. Elvis Presley did a cover; Johnny Cash did, too. And the spirit of the song lives on in much of the "praise music" popular with people who want their hearts warmed. So, even though "In the Garden" isn't a favorite anymore, the spirit of it lives on.

It was written by the prolific C. Austin Miles, and it was originally published all the way back in 1913. I was told by an apologist for the song that Miles had the encounter between Mary and the risen Lord in John's Gospel in mind when he wrote it. That may be true, and that indeed is the passage that's referenced in the hymnal that I referred to when I looked up the song. But that is not how the song functioned for the people I knew on Cape Cod. When they sang it, they were not singing about a garden, or even Mary; they were singing about themselves.

† C. Austin Miles, 1913, public domain.

I am ashamed to say that I never gave the song much thought until I read *The American Religion* by the Yale literary scholar Harold Bloom. It was Bloom that first brought the Gnostic undertone of "In the Garden" to my attention. For Bloom, a nominal Jew, but a very serious Gnostic of the old school (his designation, not mine), this is something to celebrate.

Just in case you are not familiar with Gnosticism, here is a brief explanation: the original Gnostics taught that the physical world was made by a clumsy and malevolent god, and that salvation consists in escaping from his creation by coming to know your true spiritual self. While most people are not Gnostics in this sense, Gnosticism-lite is pretty common. Gnosticism-lite cannot see how the physical world can communicate spiritual truths. Instead, spiritual insight is found within the garden of the heart.

Now, even if Bloom overstates his case in *The American Religion*, Miles's song, besides being cloying, is a withdrawal from the world. For the few people who are still familiar with the word piety, I am afraid it is the heart-religion of "In the Garden" that they associate with it.

If this is all that we had to go by when it comes to piety we might as well say good-riddance. But that isn't all we have to go by. In fact, "In the Garden" is a mockery of what piety once stood for. When you look into the history of the word what you actually see is something virile, even heroic.

PIETAS

Let's contrast "In the Garden" with another image, this one found on coins that Jesus and Paul could have held in their hands. On this coin we have a warrior with an elderly man on his back.* It was a picture of *pietas*—the word that is the basis of the English word "piety."

This wasn't the only image of *pietas* found on Roman coins. Another shows a woman holding a baby to her breast, yet another shows a woman pouring out a libation, and there are others. But it is the first image I intend to consider, because it performed the same mythic function for Romans as the Pilgrim landing at Plymouth Rock once performed for Americans. It is a scene from the ruin of Troy.

You may have read about the Trojan War in high school, or perhaps you've seen a movie about it. The story was immortalized by Homer in his epic poem, the *Iliad*. According to the story, after failing to penetrate Troy's impregnable wall, the Greeks appeared to give up. They mysteriously disappeared, but they left a parting gift—an enormous wooden horse. The Trojans foolishly wheel the gift

* The picture of this coin, "Julius Caesar AR denarius," is taken with thanks from Apollo Numismatics: (https://www.vcoins.com/en/stores/apollo_numismatics/12/product/julius_caesar_ar_denarius__venusaeneas__beautiful_toning/838398/Default.aspx), modified [accessed June 6, 2019].

into the city. Then, after dark, the Greeks who had been hiding in the horse get out and open the gates of Troy for their waiting comrades. Soon the alarm is sounded, but it is too late. The fighting is already moving from house to house and the city is in flames. The coin above depicts one of the Trojan heroes during that battle.

Here's the scene as described by Bernard Knox, Director Emeritus of Harvard's Center for Hellenistic Studies, "After realizing the fighting was no longer of use, that Troy was doomed, [Aeneas] carried his father, Anchises, on his shoulders out of the burning city, holding his son Ascanius by the hand, with his wife, Creusa, following behind."*

It would be hard to find a more manful image than this. It brings the firemen charging into the burning towers on 9/11 to mind. Most people would find it inspiring. It even has the potential of giving a heroic cast to the routine tasks of domestic life.

While they would have admired the picture, I don't think that this is what the preachers of my youth had in mind when they talked about piety. They talked about Bibles, and notebooks, and being alone with God, preferably in the woods on a summer day. So, what were the Romans thinking of when they called *this* piety? Here's Bernard Knox again,

* This is from the Introduction to Robert Fagles's translation (New York: Penguin Books, 2006), 13. All quotations that follow from the *Aeneid* are from the Fagles translation.

> The word *pius* does indeed refer, like its English derivative, to devotion and duty to the Divine; this is the reason cited by Poseidon in the *Iliad* for saving Aeneas from death at the hand of Achilles. And in the *Aeneid* he is always mindful of the gods, constant in prayer and thanks, and dutiful in sacrifice. But the words *pius* and *pietas* have in Latin a wider meaning. Perhaps the best English equivalent is something like "dutiful," "mindful of one's duty"—not only to the gods but also to one's family and to one's country.†

Here Knox alludes to the *Aeneid*, another epic poem, this one written by Virgil. In the first century Virgil was so important he was the court poet of Augustus, the Emperor of Rome. But Virgil didn't invent the story contained in the Aeneid: it was legendary, and it was believed to be as much a part of Rome's founding as the story of Romulus and Remus.‡

Here it is important to point out that the idea conveyed by the word *pietas* was not unique to the Romans. For example, Greeks had a word that had almost an identical meaning, and in Acts 17:23, the Apostle Paul used it to commend the Athenians. It is a form of ευσεβεω, and that word means, "to act reverently towards God, one's

† Fagles, 13.

‡ You may be familiar with Romulus and Remus; the story goes that they are descended from Aeneas. You may also know that Romulus killed Remus; more about that later.

country, magistrates, relations, and to all whom dutiful regard or reverence is due."*

What should impress us about both words is their comprehensive nature. They didn't promote a withdrawal from the world; they did just the opposite. That's because people didn't divide the world into religious and nonreligious categories. For people in the first century the world was a cosmos, a sacred order; and it was filled with other beings, some of whom were people, while others were gods. And you owed them. *Piety paid its debts.*

PIETAS AND POLITICS

I know paying your debts is not what comes to mind when we think of Rome. Instead we think of a litany of crime. A gap separated Rome's ideals from actual practice.

But many Romans admitted that. It was the very reason that they wanted piety back. You could say that they wanted to "Make Rome Pious Again."

Here's New Testament scholar T. Christopher Hoklotubbe making this very point: "Within imperial ideology, *pietas* signified a loyal devotion toward the gods, the nation, and family, which coalesced with Augustus's vision of restoring Rome's ancestral traditions and values and thus its moral grounding."†

* *A Greek-English Lexicon of the New Testament*, ed Joseph Henry Thayer (New York: Harper and Brothers, 1886), s.v. "Eusebeo," 262.

† T. Christopher Hoklotubbe, *Civilized Piety* (Waco, TX: Baylor University Press, 2017), 15.

This was the reason Augustus employed Virgil; and why, contrary to Virgil's instructions, the emperor intervened to prevent the unfinished epic from being destroyed after the poet's untimely death. Like many artists, apparently Virgil believed that an unfinished work was worse than no work at all. But Augustus had underwritten the poem as part of a program of cultural renewal following Rome's civil wars, and he intended to keep what he had paid for.

It is fashionable today to cynically dismiss the political uses of religion. But we practice something novel in the history of the world, what we call the "separation of Church and state." Romans would have considered that impious. In fact, Romans believed *pietas* justified their right to rule the world. Here's Cicero, the great orator and politician in the Roman Senate, making the case:

> . . . who, once convinced that divinity does exist, can fail at the same time to be convinced that it is by [divine] power that this great empire has been created, extended, and sustained? However good be our conceit of ourselves, conscript fathers, we have neither excelled the Spaniards in population, nor Gauls in vigor, nor Carthaginians in versatility, nor Greeks in art; but in piety, in devotion to religion [*sed pietate ac religione*], and in that special wisdom which consists in the recognition of the truth that the world is swayed and directed by divine power, we have excelled every race and every nation.[‡]

‡ Quoted in Hoklotubbe, 39.

PIETAS AT HOME

Just as there was no such things as the separation of Church and state in Rome, the boundary line between public things and private ones then was more porous than we're accustomed to. Everything was connected to everything else, from the most humble household, all the way up to the household of the gods. That's what made the *pietas* of the emperor's household a public matter. Here's a little more from Hoklotubbe for you:

> Augustus' household was also associated with *pietas* as exhibited in a relief from the Ara Pacis, which was dedicated by the Senate in 9 BCE. The depiction of the imperial family, including children, participating in a religious procession surrounded by priests and senators was potent and polysemous. Ara Pacis visually signified Augustus' house as a fount of *pietas* and "the religious center of Rome." Through the vast dissemination of such images, the people of Rome were invited to follow Augustus' paradigmatic piety and play their own role in securing the *pax Romana* through their dutiful observance of ancestral cults and their filial devotion to Augustus, the father of the nation . . . .*

The thing about *pietas* that you can't miss is its social character. It didn't isolate you; instead it bound you to everything else. It was the glue of the world: things divine and human

* Hoklotubbe, 28–29.

things, matter and spirit, the past and the future, and, as I am about to show you in some detail, the generations.

A good way to show you how far we have come from tying the generations together is by taking a look at a modern work of literature. I'm thinking of William Wordsworth's famous poem from 1802, "My Heart Leaps Up When I Behold." (The date tells us it was penned right after the American and French Revolutions.)

Wordsworth lived up to his name: he knew the worth of words, as well as their origins. We can be sure that a classically educated man like Wordsworth knew all about the ancient meaning of the word *piety*. This is why the poem is so telling. It's also very short:

> My heart leaps up when I behold
> A rainbow in the sky:
> So was it when my life began;
> So is it now I am a man;
> So be it when I shall grow old,
> Or let me die!
> The Child is father of the Man;
> And I could wish my days to be
> Bound each to each by natural piety.

Great poetry often employs familiar imagery in novel ways. And when this was written the Bible was still widely read by people who also read poetry. The poem begins with a rainbow; ironically that's a bad sign for anyone who believes in the piety of Aeneas. True, we associate rainbows with hope, but recall, in the Bible, the bow is hung in the sky after an old world has been washed away (Gen. 9:13–17). I can't help but believe that Wordsworth is celebrating the death of the old practice of piety. In the poem the Child acknowledges no debt but to himself. "The Child is the father of the Man." (Notice *father* is in the lower case.) The past has died in the waters of birth.

Which image seems more conducive to a Christian way of life to you: one in which a man has no debt but to himself, or the one we see on old Roman coins? If you favor Aeneas with his father on his back, I'm with you. I can't help wishing that we could have something of that old piety back—a piety that binds the generations together, and a whole lot more. I'd like to help revive it if I can.

3

AENEAS, ABRAHAM, AND PIETAS

THERE'S DISAGREEMENT ABOUT whether or not Christians should use pagan literature for Christian purposes, and it goes a long way back. Tertullian summed it up with the quip, "What does Athens have to do with Jerusalem?"

Even though he was probably thinking of Platonism, Augustine encouraged us to plunder pagan literature in the same way that the Israelites plundered Egypt on their way out of town. Augustine had a quip of his own, "All truth is God's truth." *Touché*, Tertullian.

I'm with Augustine; let's plunder Egyptian libraries, not burn them. We see precedent in Scripture. Paul employed this very technique at Mars Hill when he debated

Stoic and Epicurean philosophers in Athens. And missionaries ever since have been on the lookout for what C.S. Lewis called "good dreams" in order to show how the gospel can make good dreams come true.*

Now, here is the method to my madness: in this chapter the *Aeneid* and the Bible will be my dowsing rods. Where they seem to cross—where they seem to say something similar—I'll stop and consider what it could mean. That may sound like I'm superimposing the *Aeneid* onto the Bible, but my purpose is just the opposite. I hope to show you things in the Bible that you may have missed.

So, let's begin with mission statements. In the *Aeneid*, Aeneas had one.

His story begins *in medias res*. After the fall of Troy, some Trojan survivors escape by sea, but eventually they find themselves caught in a storm that has been stirred up by their old nemesis, the goddess Juno. After Neptune, the god of the sea, comes to the rescue, Aeneas anchors off the coast of Libya, not far from Carthage.† When he comes ashore, his mother, the goddess Venus, appears to him disguised as a huntress.

Ironically, she's the one who asks, "Who are you?"

* A fairly well-known example is found in *Peace Child* by Don Richardson.

† The episode that follows ends badly. Dido, the queen of Carthage, falls deeply in love with Aeneas. When Aeneas is compelled by Jupiter to resume his journey, Dido commits suicide. This serves as a backstory for the historic antagonism between Carthage and Rome. The hostility only ends when Rome finally destroys Carthage in the same way that Troy came to its end.

Here is his reply: "I am Aeneas, duty-bound. I carry aboard my ships the gods of house and home we seized from enemy hands. My fame goes past the skies. I seek my homeland—Italy—born as I am from highest Jove."‡

Now *that* is a mission statement. It's not the sort of thing you see in corporate America, with all the lifeless, politically correct boilerplate. It could only belong to a hero. And Aeneas is precisely that, but he didn't give this mission to himself; it was impressed upon him during the sack of Troy. First, his mother appeared to him in glory to tear him away from fighting so that he could save his family. Then later, after he's been separated from his wife Creusa in the confusion, he goes back into the burning city to find her. But instead of finding her, her ghost finds him. And after seeing his tears for her, this is what Creusa says:

> My dear husband, why so eager to give yourself
> to such mad flights of grief? It's not without
> the will of the gods that these things have come to pass.
> But the gods forbid you to take Creusa with you, ...
> The king of lofty Olympus
> won't allow it. A long exile is your fate . . .
> the vast plains of the sea are yours to plow
> until you reach Hesperian land, where Lydian Tiber
> flows . . . .
> There great joy and a kingdom
> are yours to claim, and a queen to make your wife.§

‡ Fagles, 60.

§ Fagles, 101–102.

This is one of the greatest scenes in Western literature. Centuries later it moved Saint Augustine deeply. In his *Confessions*, while recalling his youthful distaste for school, he says, "but sweet were the visions of absurdity—the wooden horse cargoed with men, Troy in flames, Creusa herself ghosting by."*

I hope this reminds you of something similar in the Bible. It is a different mission, and it is given to an unlikely hero. And this time the speaker is not a ghost: it is the one, true God, and He is addressing a man named Abram.

Here it is:

> Now the LORD said to Abram, "Go from your country and your kindred and your father's house to the land that I will show you. And I will make of you a great nation, and I will bless you and make your name great, so that you will be a blessing. I will bless those who bless you, and him who dishonors you I will curse, and in you all the families of the earth shall be blessed." (Gen. 12:1–3)

Can you see what Aeneas and Abram (later called Abraham) have in common? Both leave a world behind, both seek a promised land, and both will be remembered. Being remembered is more important than you may suppose. It means that your story doesn't come to an end when you do. People can get so bound up in your story

* *Confessions*, trans. Garry Willis (New York: Penguin Books, 2008), 1.IV.22.

that they hope for the same things that you hoped for, and live for the same things that you lived for.

But these are not the only things that Aeneas and Abraham had in common. In both stories there is a child of promise. When Aeneas comes home to save his family, he finds that his father Anchises is resolute to stay. Since he is unwilling to leave him behind, Aeneas prepares to return to the fighting, but his wife bars his way with their son.

Then, the following:

> So Creusa cries,
> her wails of anguish echoing through the house
> when out of the blue an omen strikes—a marvel!
> Now as we held our son between our hands
> and both our grieving faces, a tongue of fire,
> watch, flares up from the crown of Iulus' head,
> a subtle flame licking his downy hair, feeding
> around the boy's brow, and though it never harmed him,
> panicked, we rush to shake the flame from his curls
> and smother the holy fire . . . .
> But Father Anchises lifts his eyes to the stars in joy
> and stretching his hands toward the sky, sings out:
> "Almighty Jove! If any prayer can persuade you now,
> look down on us—that's all I ask—if our devotion
> has earned it, grant us another omen, Father,
> seal this first clear sign."
> No sooner said

> than an instant peal of thunder crashes on the left
> and down from the sky a shooting star comes gliding,
> trailing a flaming torch to irradiate the night.

At last Anchises is ready to go, and Aeneas says to him,

> "So come, dear father, climb up onto my shoulders!
> I will carry you on my back. This labor of love
> will never wear me down."*

Iulus's crown of fire is his promised future, and the hope it inspires changes Anchises's mind. And it strengthens Aeneas for his pious labors ahead.

The power of this scene is undeniable. Must we denounce it? Not even Augustine denounced the piety of Aeneas. And we don't have to either, if we receive it as a good dream, a harbinger of better things. And we won't be the first Christians to do so. Believe it or not, many Christians have honored Virgil as one of the great poets of Christendom. He was so important that Dante, perhaps the greatest poet of the late Middle Ages, actually has him serve as his guide to Hell in the first book of the *Divine Comedy*.

Now let's return to Abraham's story. He sets out for a promised land too, but without a son to lead. And after years of childlessness, he begins to wonder what it is all for.

Then this happens:

* Fagles, 98–99.

> Abram said, "O Lord GOD, what will you give me, for I continue childless, and the heir of my house is Eliezer of Damascus?" And Abraham said, "Behold, you have given me no offspring, and a member of my household will be my heir." And behold, the word of the LORD came to him: "This man shall not be your heir; your very own son shall be your heir." And he brought him outside and said, "Look toward heaven, and number the stars, if you are able to number them." Then he said to him, "So shall your offspring be." (Gen 15:2–5)

Then Abram is also given a sign:

> [The LORD] said to him, "Bring me a heifer three years old, a female goat three years old, a ram three years old, a turtledove, and a young pigeon." And he brought him all these, cut them in half, and laid each half over against the other . . . . As the sun was going down, a deep sleep fell on Abram. And behold, dreadful and great darkness fell upon him . . . . When the sun had gone down and it was dark, behold, a smoking fire pot and a flaming torch passed between these pieces. On that day the LORD made a covenant with Abram . . . . (Gen 15:9–18)

The sign was a cut that binds, an oath sealed in blood, a covenant that promised death for covenant breakers. That is what the severed animals on the ground indicated. A covenant breaker would be broken just like them. There are many important things that I could note here, but the most important of all is the fact that the symbols of God's presence pass between the halves alone. Christians have always believed that this is a sign that later, Immanuel, God with us, would pass through death as a substitute for covenant breakers like you and me.

But returning to Abraham's story: like Aeneas, Abraham is now a pious man; he is duty-bound, and so are his heirs. Circumcision will be the sign of their binding duty, repeated over the generations, binding the sons of Abraham to Abraham's God. And in days to come, when his heirs ask, "Who are you?" God will invariably reply, "I am the God of your fathers, the God of Abraham, Isaac, and Jacob."

Once more to the dowsing rods, as their stories are told, and as their heirs follow them, we discover another place where the stories of Aeneas and Abraham cross. In both of them, their houses win their promised lands through pious wars.

BENEFACTION

That a war could be pious is incomprehensible to many people. One of the reasons for this is that we don't feel a compelling need to provide for our heirs. Modern life is more regulated and prosperous than ancient people could have imagined. But neither Aeneas nor Abraham could take prosperity for granted. Each felt a responsibility to establish a legacy; each wanted his household to keep growing and going long after he was gone.

Our inability to understand this has something to do with the fact that people no longer see themselves as part of a line. Instead, we think of ourselves as points—disconnected, isolated, and seemingly self-contained points.*

This is probably why most people don't know their genealogies, at least not without a lot of research. But both Aeneas and Abraham believed they had received some benefit from above, and each felt duty-bound to pass it on to his heirs. This is what I mean by a legacy. You could say it was the whole point of their stories. And securing the benefits of a legacy would mean a fight in both cases.

The fact that their promised lands were already occupied complicated matters for them. Of course, when Abraham initially enters his promised land, he is in no position to force anything on anybody. Instead he strives to live in peace as a stranger in the land. The one time that we know of that he resorted to force of arms he did so in order to rescue his nephew Lot and his household. But after this episode it is back to the tents for the old Bedouin. It is only much later, when his descendants have grown numerous, that his household goes to war.

But with Aeneas the need and the manpower are there from the start.

Let's keep it real here. In any political community there is a sovereign and there are subjects. If your people live in

* Isolating people and turning them into individuals has been a central theme of political philosophy since the Enlightenment. Hobbes, Locke, Rousseau, Kant, et al. We live in their shadows, but we don't know it.

subjugation to the political order of another people, sooner or later you will find that the interests of your community and the dictates of those who govern you will come into conflict. You can avoid this by just blending in and losing your identity. That would bring an end to your people, of course. On the other hand, you could just break away, which means a fight, unless you can persuade your current ruler to let you go. (Not a given, as the heirs of Abraham learned in Egypt; but then you have to find a place to go, and vacant real estate is hard to come by.) There is a third way, but it is quite difficult, and that is by maintaining a minority status indefinitely.

Typically, power and prestige are withheld from minorities. It is true that in rare instances a minority can enjoy the favor of a sovereign, as we see with Joseph and the house of Abraham during their sojourn in Egypt. But we can also see from that episode that this is a very precarious thing, and the fortunes of a people can change with a change in the regime. What followed for the Israelites in Egypt was slavery. And this is why they made their way back to the land of promise after their deliverance.

HOW AENEAS AND ABRAHAM EVENTUALLY COME INTO CONFLICT

What keeps the stories of Aeneas and Abraham from merely being biographical is the universal scope of the promises made to them. Both were promised the world.

Naturally, if all goes well for their heirs that means that the houses of Aeneas and Abraham will eventually meet. They finally did, and, because of mutually exclusive claims of benefaction, a war followed.

AENEAS AND THE ROMAN WAY OF PIOUS WAR

For most modern readers, the best part of the *Aeneid* is the first half, but for Romans it may have been the other way around. Everything in the story builds to a fight.

When the Trojans finally arrive in Italy, the feelings of the locals are mixed, unsurprisingly. When their king offers his daughter to Aeneas in order to unite the strength of their houses, her former suitor Turnus is outraged, and he musters an army to win her.

As the story unfolds, it is clear that this fight stands for something more. You could say that it is a prelude for coming attractions.

To prepare her son for the fight, Venus persuades her husband Vulcan to make Aeneas a suit of armor. And the most important thing that he makes for him is a shield, prophetically emblazoned with the story of Aeneas' ever-victorious children in years to come.

Here's Virgil:

> Such vistas
> the God of Fire forged across the shield
> that Venus gives her son. He fills with wonder

> — he knows nothing of these events but takes delight
> in their likeness, lifting onto his shoulders now
> the fame and fates of all his children's children.*

Did you notice a subtle shift here? Having figuratively set his father down after his death earlier in the story, Aeneas now takes up his armor to wage war for his children's children.

Paradoxically, from the Roman point of view, this is a blessing for the world. Romans justified their conquests as the progress of peace. They called it the *Pax Romana*—the Peace of Rome. Virgil has Anchises give the Romans their charge from the land of the dead:

> "But you, Roman, remember, rule with all your power
> the peoples of the earth—these will be your arts:
> to put your stamp on the works and ways of peace,
> to spare the defeated, break the proud in war."†

Empire builders always justify their conquests like this. And in a way, they've got a point. We don't cherish the artifacts of small kingdoms in the same way that we do the works of great civilizations. Recall, upon coming down to inspect the Tower of Babel the LORD makes this observation, "Behold, they are one people . . . this is only the

* Fagles, 265.
† Fagles, 210.

beginning . . . . And nothing that they propose to do will now be impossible for them" (Gen. 11:6).

Augustine began his defense of the City of God by quoting the very words of Anchises above. But he rejects the piety of the *Pax Romana*; instead insisting that Rome was founded on fratricide. Romulus should get the credit, a man, like Cain, who killed his brother and then built a city.

But Augustine said that in the fifth century. The *Aeneid* was published in the first. The civil strife that brought the Caesars to power had cut the thread that had held an older way of way of life together. It was a critical moment. The emperor's program of cultural renewal not only included the *Aeneid*, it also included a huge investment in temple building, and the promotion of the cult of the emperor. And there were new laws to strengthened the institution of traditional marriage among the elite. Vigorous promotion of Roman piety was imperial policy.

Nevertheless, cults from the East used Roman roads to spread throughout the empire. And on those roads also traveled a descendant of Abraham who would prove to be a match for Virgil and his epic poem.

THE HEIRS OF ABRAHAM AND THEIR PIOUS WARS

In the first century, the house of Abraham looked like it had failed to live up to its promise. According to the record we have in Joshua and Judges, the conquest of their promised land was at best a partial success. They never fully occupied it, and the House of David, its most successful dynasty, lost its northern territory after only two generations. Then one empire after another swept over the divided kingdom, and by the first century the northern kingdom was long gone. All that remained of it was a region inhabited by a motley band of syncretists, and some intrepid colonists from the south who had carved out a home in a place called Galilee.

Eventually the inexorable might of Rome arrived and Judea was brought into the *Pax Romana*. Then Rome did what it always did, and powerful nations still do today because it often works: they set up a puppet ruler. The Roman Senate, in a surprise move, made Herod king of Judea in 40 BC. What followed was a period of prosperity and the construction of vast public works, the largest being the renovation and expansion of the temple in Jerusalem.

Nevertheless, for pious Jews, the situation was intolerable. Herod's claim to the kingship had no basis. He wasn't of the line of David, and because he was duty-bound to Rome, the Jewish nation was *de facto* an unwilling a participant in the idolatry of the Roman state.

Yet, in spite of all that, the hope of national sovereignty lived on, largely because of prophecies that promised a Messiah that would restore the kingdom to Israel, and not only take back its land, but actually fill the entire world with the kingdom of God.*

Messianic fever was running hot in the first century, and would-be Messiahs appeared from time to time, as Gamaliel noted in his speech to the Sanhedrin in the Book of Acts. But eventually the unrest grew so great that Roman legions arrived to pacify the Jews. The siege of Jerusalem brought about the destruction of the temple and a great diaspora of Jews across the Roman world. Today, all that remains of the temple is a portion of its foundation. But in Rome, the Arch of Titus was erected and in its reliefs the spoils from the temple are depicted in a Roman triumph.

But before the fall of Jerusalem a man named Jesus of Nazareth appeared. Some of Abraham's children believed that He was the promised Messiah. But the Jewish leaders rejected Him and handed Him over to the Romans to be crucified.

Then there was a sudden, joyous turn: Jesus rose bodily from the dead, demonstrating that He actually was the promised Messiah, and by implication, the heir of the entire world.

The people who had believed in Him were radicalized because the resurrection demonstrated that not even death could stand in the way of the kingdom of God. Then, in the household of a Roman centurion another sign followed that indicated that anyone who wanted to join Abraham's household would be welcome to, so long as

* Isaiah 9:6–7—just one of many such prophecies.

he believed that Jesus rose from the dead (Acts 10).* These people came to be called Christians (Acts 11:26).

At this point a new phase in the conflict between Aeneas and Abraham begins. And to anyone on the ground in the first century, the eventual outcome could not have been imagined. Because in the end, the Christian way of war actually won, and even the Roman Emperor submitted to another peace when it was over, the *Pax Christi*. Here's the poet Prudentius, from the fifth century: "Now the successor of Aeneas, in the imperial purple, prostrates himself in prayer at the house of Christ, and the supreme lord adores the banner of the cross."†

Instrumental in this victory was the Apostle Paul, the first great theologian of Christianity. He was uniquely equipped for the task. He was actually a dual citizen—a descendant of Abraham, an heir by birth, and a Roman citizen by law. He was also an intellectual, having been a student of Gamaliel, the most renowned rabbi of the day.

What he outlined was a new mode of pious warfare, something that I believe could be called *guerrilla piety*. And along with this new mode of warfare he identified a new field of conflict. It wasn't the Jewish homeland, or even the lands subject to Rome. The field of conflict was the cosmos itself.

* Just before this incident, a cripple named Aeneas is healed by Peter (Acts 9:32-35). Coincidence?

† Prudentius, *Vol. I*, trans. H.J. Thomson, Loeb Classic Library (Cambridge: Harvard University Press, 1949), 155.

PART TWO:

THE WAR FOR THE COSMOS

4

WAGING PEACE

PAUL'S EPISTLE TO THE EPHESIANS HAS been admired by heavenly-minded people. Coleridge called it "the divinest composition of man."*

This is why it may come as a surprise that the letter ends in an alarming way. It ends with this:

> Finally, be strong in the Lord and in the strength of his might. Put on the whole armor of God, that you may be able to stand against the schemes of the devil. For we do not wrestle against flesh and blood, but against the rulers, against the authorities, against the cosmic powers over this present darkness, against the spiritual forces of evil in the heavenly places.

* S.T. Coleridge, *Table Talk*, May 25, 1830, quoted in Andrew T. Lincoln, *Ephesians: A Word Biblical Commentary* (Waco, TX: Word Books, 1990).

> Therefore take up the armor of God, that you may be able to withstand in the evil day, and having done all, to stand firm. Stand therefore, having fastened on the belt of truth, and having put on the breastplate of righteousness, and, as shoes for your feet, having put on the readiness given by the gospel of peace. In all circumstances take up the shield of faith, with which you can extinguish all the flaming darts of the evil one; and take the helmet of salvation, and the sword of the Spirit, which is the word of God, praying at all times in the Spirit, with all prayer and supplication. To that end, keep alert with all perseverance, making supplication for all the saints, and also for me, that words may be given to me in opening my mouth boldly to proclaim the mystery of the gospel, for which I am an ambassador in chains, that I may declare it boldly, as I ought to speak. (Eph. 6:10–20)

When this passage is addressed by commentators, it seldom is addressed as the thing that Paul has been driving at from the start. Usually it is treated as an addendum, something like, "Oh, and by the way, you know that I'm in prison, and I just noticed how one of my guards is dressed, and it made me think of this."

The reason for this is the way that we read the Bible. We hop from here to there, looking for inspiration to get through the day. But that's a formula for taking things out of context. If you can, you should be read it all at once—as a whole. If you do, you'll see that Ephesians builds to a fight, just like we saw in the *Aeneid.*

In the early chapters, Paul shows us what we're up against and how our Lord fought for us. Now Paul says, it's your turn.

So, Ephesians is a handbook for guerrilla piety. In this chapter, and those that follow, I will largely stick to his strategy. It is my belief that since it worked once, it can work again. I don't suppose guerrilla piety like this was the sort of thing you thought you were signing up for when you became a Christian. You were probably told that Christianity is a walk in the garden with Jesus, or the purpose driven life, or even your best life now.

I feel like a drill sergeant breaking the news to new recruits when they get off the bus. I'm saying in effect, "I don't care that the recruiter told you that you'd see the world or get money for college; this is the Marine Corps, and we fight to win."

Before I dive into the subject of why we fight, here is a warning: This is serious. It is the sort of thing that can land you in prison. As I just noted, Paul actually wrote Ephesians in a prison. Have you ever wondered why Marines never smile for the photographer when their portraits are taken at the end of boot camp? It is because they aren't used car salesmen looking forward to their best life now. They're prepared to do their duty. And when we see their photographs in the news, it may be because they are in a prison camp, or worse.

So, what are we fighting for? Well, we're not fighting for real estate in the Middle East. We're not fighting for an empire, either—or any human institution, no matter how big it is. We're fighting for *everything* there is. We're fighting for the cosmos.

WELCOME TO THE COSMOS

When people use the word *cosmos* today they tend to use it as a synonym for the word *universe*. But the words don't actually convey the same idea, as people can see if they look into the origins of the words. *Universe* stresses the singleness of reality—that we live in something that turns as a whole. It's a fine word, even though we've forgotten its meaning. Similarly, most people have no clue when it comes to the origin of the word *cosmos*.

The reason has a lot to do with the pop science on display in an old PBS television series that was actually entitled *Cosmos*. I can recall the sensation that the original broadcast created. It was something of a coming out party for celebrity scientist and atheist Carl Sagan.

Sagan revealed the hidden agenda that informed the series when he famously intoned in the introduction, "The Cosmos is all that is or was or ever will be. Our feeblest contemplations of the Cosmos stir us—there is a tingling in the spine, a catch in the voice, a faint sensation, as if a distant memory, of falling from a height. We know we are approaching the greatest of mysteries."

It was a very clever opening, and we should give Sagan credit. But we should also note that he plagiarized it. It was an echo of the words of Christ in Revelation, "'I am the Alpha and the Omega,' says the Lord God, 'who is and who was and who is to come, the Almighty'" (Rev. 1:8). But we should also hear a little of Paul in it as well. In fact, we should hear something that reminds us of Ephesians.

This brings me back to the origin of the word *cosmos*. In the first century, it was a way of seeing shared by Christians and their pagan neighbors. You will need to keep it in view if you hope to see the point of this chapter, and of this entire book.

Paul and his Roman audience didn't see the cosmos in the same way that Carl Sagan did. The cosmos was more than matter in motion for them. It was an ordered thing—the largest order of them all. That's what the word actually meant. It included everything, even invisible things. And it also housed microcosms—little orders that depended on and reflected the larger one. If they didn't, they couldn't exist.

In case you're wondering why this has even come up at this point, it is because Paul used the word in Ephesians 1:4. The word that is translated with the English word *world* is actually *cosmos* in the Greek. It's a shame that the word *world* doesn't bring *order* to mind. When we use it we generally mean *this place where we live*, or we use it synonymously with *earth*. For a reason that remains a mystery, but we can be grateful for nonetheless, the English Standard Version does translate it in the right way in Ephesians 6:12 when it takes the form of an adjective, *cosmic*.

But there is something ironic about the way we use the word *cosmos* today, because in a real way, what we mean by it is almost the opposite of what it used to mean. When Sagan insisted that the cosmos is all there is, he explicitly rejected the ancient view that an order depended on an order-giver. Instead, Sagan tried to explain how matter can order itself, without the benefit of intelligence. Following this line of reasoning, the word *cosmos* is more like a misleading metaphor.

Now, some people in the past believed that the cosmos took its present form through a violent process.* In those stories the gods fight to impose an order on a rival order or on plain old chaos. (On a side note, if you won't have intelligent design, then the semblance of order can only come about through a violent process. Think of Darwin's mechanism of natural selection, or the Big Bang.)

With the gods of antiquity, order was called for so that the gods could have a suitable place to live. This captures a valuable insight that is reflected in the Latin word for house—the word *domus*. Not only is that the root of the word *domestic*, it is also the root of the word *dominion*. In the same way, the cosmos is like a great house, one that is divinely ordered.

Certainly we see this in Christianity. But biblical cosmogony is different in important respects from other creation stories. For one thing it is not a violent process but

* For example: Zeus and company and the Titans. There are many others.

proceeds in a much more workmanlike way. God is not imposing His will on something resistant. Instead He made a pliable material out of nothing with which He forms a cosmos (Heb. 11:3). But it is what biblical cosmogony has in common with all the others that I want you to see. When it came to the cosmos, Christians and their neighbors agreed that there was someone in heavenly places giving orders.

VERTICALITY

Speaking of the heavens, the ancient cosmos always had a top. Sagan's cosmos doesn't come with a top. It has no normative vertical dimension whatsoever. It is just space, as in outer space. Paradoxically, this means Sagan's cosmos is flat, because without verticality it is impossible to make meaningful distinctions or say that some things are more important than other things. Sagan, who liked to wax poetic, was known for referring to his viewers as "star stuff." Just why this should flatter anyone remains unexplained. Frogs and rocks are star stuff too.

What this reveals is that the only way Sagan's cosmos can be given any charm at all is by sneaking in a little of the old cosmos here and there. According to the old way of seeing things, stars are a lot more than stuff. We get a little glimpse of just how rich, and even personal, the cosmos could be for people in the past when we read books like *The Voyage of the Dawn Treader* by C.S. Lewis. In that book, a youthful version of Sagan by the name of Eustace

Clarence Scrub remarks when he meets a star in person, "In our world a star is a huge ball of flaming gas." To this the star replies, "Even in your world, my son, that is not what a star is, but only what it is made of."*

Even today we know in our bones that the cosmos comes with a top, but we can't explain why we should feel this way. The reason is we've been taught to separate facts from values. Facts are "out there" for all to see, but values are things that just exist in our heads. They're subjective.

When it comes to the cosmos, being high meant you had oversight. (It's what it means to be an overseer: you're higher in a hierarchy.) And being low meant looking up to your rulers, as when someone says of someone he admires, "I really look up to him." Now, here's some more etymology: *hierarchy* means sacred rule, *hieros*, for *sacred*, and *arch*, for *ruler*.

And we have all of this in Ephesians. We have heavenly places (1:3, 1:20, 2:6, 3:10) and we have the regions below (1:20, 2:1, 4:9). And Christ has traveled the intervening span (4:8-10). But it is the inbetween space that should interest us for at least a couple of reasons: first, because it is a problem (1:21, 2:2, 6:12), and second, because we live there. Interestingly, J.R.R. Tolkien and C.S. Lewis, drawing on Norse mythology, had a name for it. They called it Middle Earth.

* *The Voyage of the Dawn Treader* (1980; New York: HarperCollins Publishers, 1952), 227. What Lewis demonstrates in this amusing encounter is that some people actually believed that a star was an intelligent body of some kind. They even believed that they had biblical warrant for this (1 Cor. 15:40ff).

So the cosmos isn't empty space, it's layered.† And on our level, we are not the only occupants. Just a little above us, there are principalities and powers. And we're not just talking about City Hall. Paul actually names their chief: "the Prince of the Power of the Air." (No elected official that I know of actually goes by that name, although some of them act as if they did.) What a marvelous moniker, and apt too; the reference to air conveys the sense of being immersed, surrounded by a realm that is ruled by a spirit that is as real, yet as invisible, as air.

The problem with this layer of the cosmos is that its prince is insubordinate. The layer that we live in is like a province ruled by an ambitious and wily governor. People living in it don't necessarily know this, although they feel the effects of the conflict. According to Paul, this layer of the cosmos will eventually be brought to heel beneath the feet of Christ (1:22).

We tend to write off Paul's words about "principalities and powers" as just a bunch of poetry, if we think about them at all. Oddly, many Christians today agree with Sagan that science gives us the cosmos as it is. What Christianity adds is Jesus in your heart.

But this is unacceptable. It not only downgrades the cosmos and the Lordship of Christ, it doesn't even do justice to poetry.

† Even heaven is layered, we can see that in Paul's reference to a "third heaven" (2 Cor. 12:2).

SPEAKING UP FOR POETRY

Please forgive this little detour, but it's important.

Poetry wasn't always self-indulgent. It was once believed that it could tell truths about the real world that could *only* be told poetically. The reality that poetry is best suited to speak of is invisible reality, reality that can't be counted, or measured, or boiled over a Bunsen burner. And people believed this because they knew something about language that has been lost to most of us. They believed that human language has its origin in the language that spoke the cosmos into being (Gen. 1, John 1).

To this way of thinking, knowledge and language go together hand in glove. As I mentioned before, we can see it in the Greek word *logos*—a word that can be translated either as *word* or as *reason* because it means both at the same time. The connection between language and the cosmos can be seen in both Testaments of the Bible: in the Old, when we hear the words, "And God said, " (Gen 1:3), and in the New we read the words, "In the beginning was the Word (logos)," (John 1:1) Put those verses together and you can see that the Word is behind the order of things.

It was once even believed that the language of creation was the language used by Adam to name the animals in paradise (Gen. 2:19). Just what could that have sounded like? The third book of C.S. Lewis's space trilogy, *That Hideous Strength* contains a suggestion. In that book we follow a small band of eccentric scholars fighting against the forces of evil. One of those scholars is an authority in ancient languages, and his name is Dimble. In the following scene he speaks and the world moves.

Listen to this:

> And Dimble . . . raised his head, and great syllables of words that sounded like castles came out of his mouth. Jane felt her heart leap and quiver at them. Everything else in the room seemed to have been intensely quiet; even the bird, and the bear, and the cat, were still, staring at the speaker. The voice did not sound like Dimble's own: it was as if the words spoke themselves through him from some strong place at a distance—or as if they were not words at all but present operations of God . . . . For this was the language spoken before the Fall and beyond the Moon, and the meanings were not given to the syllables by chance, or skill, or long tradition, but truly inherent in them as the shape of the great Sun is inherent in the little waterdrop.*

Today we don't look into the origins of words for insight. We rely on mathematics for that. We can see something of the transition in the following quotation from Galileo,

> Philosophy is written in that great book which ever lies before our eyes—I mean the universe—but we cannot understand it if we do not first learn the language and grasp the symbols, in which it is written. This book is written in the mathematical language, and the symbols are triangles, circles and other geometrical figures, without whose help

* *That Hideous Strength* (1974; New York: Scribner, 1945), 225–226.

> it is impossible to comprehend a single word of it; without which one wanders in vain through a dark labyrinth.*

What distinguishes spoken words from mathematics is what they can communicate. For words to exist you need a speaker. But when it comes to numbers, a machine can do the job. Since atheists don't believe that the cosmos has a maker, they prefer counting things to pondering the meaning of things.† The problem with this is they can't account for human intelligence in this manner. They assume that the human brain is just a computer and the mind is its software. That's why materialists in Silicon Valley believe that computers will become conscious when they can compute large amounts of data fast enough.‡

But let's get back to the first century, when people had a little more sense. Paul preached Christ as the meaning maker of the cosmos. When He won His victory over the Prince of the Power of the Air when He was raised from

* *The Assayer* (1623), trans. Thomas Salusbury (1661), as quoted in Edwin Arthur Burtt, *The Metaphysical Foundations of Modern Science* (New York: Dover Publications, 2003), 75.

† Math isn't diabolical, it reflects the glory of God in its own way. My friend Tony Esolen reminded me recently that many of the greats in the field were deeply Christian. He also noted something that I've actually heard mathematicians say, almost all of them at Platonists: The thing to remember about Platonists is they believe that unseen things are real in a deeper and more profound way than the things that we can see and count.

‡ Jaron Lanier, *You Are Not a Gadget: A Manifesto* (New York: Vintage Books, 2010). Lanier is a Silicon Valley insider turned heretic. His argument can be summed up simply: You never get from quantity to quality.

the dead and ascended to His heavenly throne, things began to be reordered to their given ends in Him.

And it is because of this that there is something for us to do.

CONTESTED BENEFITS

Even though Christians and their pagan neighbors agreed that there was someone behind the order of things, they disagreed about the identity of that someone. And it was important enough to them to fight about it.

For people that believe in the separation of Church and state, this seems odd. Why would they fight about *that*? It comes down to paying your debts.

From time to time in the Old Testament, the LORD takes the trouble to remind people of all the things that He has done for them. There is hardly an instance in which He says, "Just do it because I said so." His commands are often justified by some version of, "After all that I've done for you." Here's a prominent example of what I mean. It comes from the prelude to the Ten Commandments. "I am the LORD your God, who brought you out of the land of Egypt, out of the house of slavery" (Deut. 5:6).

Beneath the surface of biblical law, what you find is a tacit definition of equity as justice. People, and God, should get what they deserve. I suppose you could call it a natural law, because it is difficult to imagine how social creatures anywhere, at any time, could live without it. It should be obvious that God doesn't need you and me, but it should be just as obvious that we need Him. And the pious response to all that God has done for us is grateful submission to His law.

So, it should not surprise us that Roman piety has that basis. It begins with benefaction. An elaborate hierarchy of patronage is what bound Roman social life together. It began with the gods and trickled down from there. Everyone was duty-bound in some way in this vast structure.

So far, so good, Christian piety and Roman piety had the same basis in gratitude. But hopefully you can see why this is also the problem. Remember, Romans, and Gentiles generally speaking, also believed that they owed gratitude to their gods. They had debts to pay, too. So, if different, mutually exclusive deities each claim credit for the good things in life, to whom do you address payment?

For Christians, Rome's gods were idols at best, demons in disguise at worst. This doesn't mean that they thought Rome's rule had nothing to justify it. Paul said that every governing authority was God's servant, whether the authority knew it or not. But Christians could not submit to the deities that Romans claimed justified their authority. Not only were they forbidden to, doing so would be lying.

HOW CHRISTIANITY RAISED THE STAKES

The benefits Christians claimed to enjoy were at one and the same time more tremendous and more personal than anything anyone else claimed to enjoy. This meant that, whatever the Romans claimed, Christ's claim was stronger (Rom. 1:4). Paul addresses the Ephesians as though they know exactly what he is talking about. The one true God is their Father (1:2), and they are His adopted sons (1:5), their sins have been forgiven (1:7), and on top of all this, they have received an inheritance (1:11, 18; 3:6). These references are all set within the framework of a household order (2:19). And remarkably, they've done nothing to deserve being treated in this way. It is entirely by grace (2:8–9).

As good as it all sounds, it is set within an even larger frame of reference than it is possible for us to fully appreciate. The frame of reference is nothing less than the cosmos itself (1:4).* Here's Paul in Colossians, showing why Christ has a higher claim on human gratitude than anyone else:

> He is the image of the invisible God, the firstborn of all creation. For by him all things were created, in heaven and on earth, visible and invisible, whether thrones or dominions or rulers or authorities—all things were created through him and for him. And he is before all things, and in him all things hold together. And he is the head of the body, the church. He is the beginning, the firstborn from the dead, that in everything he might be preeminent. For in him all the fullness of God was pleased to dwell, and through him to reconcile to himself all things, whether on

* *Kosmou*, meaning world.

earth or in heaven, making peace by the blood of his cross. (Col. 1:15–20)

In this profound passage we're told that Jesus is far more than our personal savior. He is the Lord of the Cosmos.

WAGING PEACE

There are many paradoxes in the world. One is the adage, *if you want peace, prepare for war*. Some people don't believe in paradoxes. They're idealists. You just need to plan your work: it's all flow-charts, and mission statements, and getting the right laws passed, and then everything is hunky-dory.

Romans were not idealists. They were realists. They dealt with the situation on the ground; and when it came to troops on the ground, Rome was tough to beat. The Jews tried and lost badly. The Roman war wagon rolled right over them and kept on going.

Before that, Rome had brutally gotten its own house in order. The Republic had been constitutionally incapable of keeping the peace over the vast territory it ruled. Standing armies were financed directly by their generals. Civil war had been practically inevitable. In the end Augustus defeated his rivals, and from that point on there was no going back to the old way of doing things.

From the perspective of the people on the ground, this was a good thing. The triumph of Augustus was celebrated in works of art, among them, the *Gemma Augustea*, a carving dated from the second or third decade of the first century AD, not long before Paul wrote to the Ephesians.* The gem shows Augustus seated in a heavenly place. We know it is a heavenly place because he is surrounded by gods. And that goddess in the background holding a laurel over his head, is none other than Οικουμενη, the goddess of the inhabited world. I hope that you can see what this implies about the peace of Christ. Christians believed

* Image thanks to Wikipedia, s.v. "Gemma Augustea," last modified March 9, 2019, q6:03, https://en.wikipedia.org/wiki/Gemma_Augustea. Photo by James Steakley—Self-photographed, October 2013 (James Steakley), CCBY-SA 3.0, https://commons.wikimedia.org/w/index.php?curid=30890931, modified (b&w, background edited out).

that Christ was Lord in a way that Romans believed that Augustus was Lord. He had made rebellious authorities submit, and he was now seated in a heavenly place. And he also governed a capacious household where former enemies lived together in peace.

In Christ's house the dividing wall of hostility between Jew and Gentile had come down. But it wasn't accomplished by blending two religious systems with their respective gods. On the contrary, there was a clear winner. The principalities and powers had rebelled, but Christ had risen victorious over them. Now the covenant promises that bound the Jews were opened to receive the Gentiles. And a great house, an οικουμενη, a habitation for all people, had been formed (Eph. 2:19).

If you're ready to join the fight at this point, you should find your place to start. That's what I intend to help you with in the next chapter.

5

LOST AND FOUND IN THE COSMOS

WALKER PERCY WROTE A BOOK AMUSingly titled *Lost in the Cosmos: The Last Self-Help Book.*[*] In part it was inspired by Sagan's aforementioned PBS series, *Cosmos*. But it was also a send-up of the conceit of self-help books. The subtitle of Percy's book could have read, "How to help yourself when you don't know where you are, or even what you are."

Percy knew that our troubles didn't begin with modern science. They have more to do with human nature and the way we get things wrong in uniquely modern ways. For example, one of the truly odd things about

* New York: Picador, 2000; originally published Farrar, Straus, and Giroux, 1983.

modern philosophy is something called "the state of nature." When philosophers employed the term back in the seventeenth and eighteenth centuries, they didn't actually mean what scientists are talking about when they discuss their observations. What these modern philosophers did was actually very unnatural. They tried conceptually to isolate individuals from the communities that they are born into. At first, this was done in order to understand why individuals should want to live in political communities. But it soon developed into a way to liberate people from the constraints of social institutions in general, such as households, for example.

The conceit was that you didn't need to begin with God if you could find another starting point. This was the approach to everything in modern philosophy. If you have ever taken a course in modern philosophy, you know how odd it can be. Many people point to Rene Descartes as the man who got it all going. Basically Descartes said that the only thing you can really be sure of is your own consciousness. That's what his famous dictum, "I think therefore I am" is getting at. Here's another way of putting it: Descartes didn't think you could really know anything outside your head.

However, your head is not where the Bible begins. One of my favorites passages making this point is found in Exodus. There we see Moses before the burning bush. When Moses asks, "Who are you?" The voice of the LORD replies from the bush, "I AM," (Exod. 3:14). Theologians up until just yesterday believed that this is the most basic form of knowledge, and that everything else logically follows from it. And Scripture tells us as much elsewhere, "The fear of the LORD is the beginning of wisdom" (Prov. 9:10).

The Bible reflects an order that exists outside of its pages. Reality begins with God, and lesser things follow. Seeing this was once largely a matter of common sense. For instance, one common sense observation was that no one actually makes himself. Since that's the case, the wise tried to see where God placed individuals in the natural order of things, the assumption being that since God is good, the environments that He puts things in naturally help them to flourish.

So they began with the most natural social group, the household, and went from there. Next came the village. Then when you have several villages that can be bound together you have something called a *polis*.* Then there was the largest order of all, the cosmos. We can imagine it as a set of Russian nesting dolls. The cosmic macrocosm, and concentric microcosms nesting within it, until you get to the smallest microcosms of all—you and me.†

So, the ancients were definitely *not* lost in the cosmos. The thought would have been absurd to them. People belong to a natural order, and they believed that human

* Aristotle, *Politics*.

† Harry O. Maier in *New Testament Christianity in the Roman World* (New York: Oxford University Press, 2018) uses this very image of nesting dolls (24).

communities were natural. And they believed that the first community is the household.

JUST WHAT IS A HOUSEHOLD?

If I were to sum up this book with a single idea it would be this: household piety is as big as the cosmos. It connects you to everything because it is at the center of everything else.

I've talked about piety, and I've talked about the cosmos. Now it is time to talk about households. But before I can do that, I still have a lot of explaining to do, because if I don't miss my guess, you are probably still in the dark as to what a household actually is.

To begin, imagine a world without business corporations, or social welfare agencies, or factories, or daycare centers. Where do you suppose people made a living, or found help when they needed it? In their households, naturally. Now, let that sink in for a moment.

Okay, what can we conclude from this? First of all, a household wasn't a building. It wasn't even a family—although it certainly included one. Essentially a household was an authority structure.

The reason that authority was essential was because a household was an *economy*. The etymology of that word tells a story. It is derived from two Greek words, *oikos*, meaning *house*, and *nomos*, meaning law; an economy was *the law of the house*. It directed the labors of its members toward their common good; it's what kept people working together.

Household economies were based on some productive enterprise, usually farming, or a trade. Sometimes they were subsistence economies—where people eked out a living. Other times they produced goods for the market. Either way, in the premodern world, households were nearly the only thing going. They produced food, clothing, and nearly everything else worth having. And on top of that, they were social welfare agencies, educating the young, and caring for the elderly. People depended on them for almost everything.

Today we largely think of our homes as recreation centers. That's because in the Industrial Revolution most of the productive economy moved out of the house. Because of this, some people have wondered, just what is a father for?*

But in the first century a father's authority was unquestioned. People just depended on him for so much that life without him was hard to imagine. He adjudicated household disputes; in a world where the police were never a phone call away, he defended and enforced its boundaries. And he spoke for the household's interests in public forums. A father was so important, his untimely death often led to the breaking up of a household and the distribution of its members to his relations.

* I discuss in more detail how to recover a productive household, with its roles and functions, in my book *Man of the House* (Eugene, OR: Wipf and Stock, 2017)..

XENOPHON'S GUIDEBOOK

We have a library of resource books from antiquity on the subject of the household economy, so the general state of ignorance on the subject in our time can't be blamed on a lack of information. One of my go-to resources comes from the fourth century BC. It is Xenophon's Socratic dialogue, Οικονομικος, sometimes rendered in English as *The Estate Manager*. Unfortunately, something very important was lost in translation here. The Greek word for *household* is right there in the title. So, if anyone were to ask me for my translation, here's how I would render it instead: *The House Steward.*

Xenophon was an ancient philosopher with a practical cast of mind. Socrates, as you may recall, was also a philosopher—but he is often accused of having his head in the clouds. However, in this dialogue, Xenophon includes Socrates as a character—just like he is in Plato's dialogues. But in these dialogues there isn't much action. Instead, you're listening in on very deep conversations. And the hope is that you will learn something by eavesdropping.

In this particular dialogue, Socrates interviews two men. In the first interview we see him stinging the pride of a wealthy and incompetent fellow by the name of Critobulus. Despite his wealth and his vast estate, he is running in the red because his property is poorly managed. Socrates suggests that he should find someone who can manage his affairs for him. This leads to a conversation about who has the best reputation for household management in Athens. A name comes up, and Socrates sets out to see if he can learn something from him. Once he finds him, the remaining two-thirds of the dialogue is given to this interview.

It turns out that the man's name is Ischomachus. In most Socratic dialogues, Socrates is a very sage if somewhat annoying conversationalist who is adept at pointing out the weaknesses in his interlocutor's arguments. But for perhaps the only time in any Socratic dialogue, we see Socrates play the fawning acolyte here. What follows is something like an instruction manual consisting of questions from Socrates and the sturdy answers Socrates gratefully receives.

The subjects addressed include: agriculture and husbandry, training and working with servants, the work of the wife and how it complements the work of the husband as head of house, the ways one can build competence and loyalty among those who work for the owners of the household, and finally, how to build wealth over the long-term. Good planning, self-control, and piety are the themes that tie it all together.

If some of this sounds somewhat familiar, this is because it is still with us, just applied to small businesses, or the self-help literature Walker Percy made fun of. What has been almost entirely lost, though, is its basis in the household, especially as it was developed as a natural outworking of the union of a husband and wife.

Most books on marriage today, even those published by Christian authors, never get close to the household economy as it was practiced throughout the ancient world, and as it was described in the Bible. What we generally get instead is the deconstructed household that doesn't reflect much beyond the desires of the couple that make it up from scratch.*

BEFORE THE PATRIARCH GOT TIPPED

In the pre-modern world, a father gave his household its vertical dimension. That's because you must have hierarchy when serious work is to be done. But verticality didn't begin or end with him. Fathers were subject to higher authorities. You could call them the middlemen of the cosmos. He stands between his household and heaven, representing each to the other.

Heavenly laws were the real basis of the economy; the welfare of a household depended on them. That's why a pious man enforced them. He was embedded in a structure he did not invent, and he had responsibilities that he did not choose. Piety consisted in performing his duty.

As you know, things are different today. Households are not economies in the old sense of the term; they're actually more like recreation centers. We've outsourced productive enterprise to the workplace, and when it comes to social welfare, now the young, the old, the sick, and the out of work, all depend on the helping professions.

* Examples of the thing I describe could fill a library.

The unexpected consequence of this has been a downgrade in a father's authority. Unexpected, that is, by anyone who isn't a Marxist; Marx saw it coming and rejoiced. In our time just what is a father supposed to be in charge of, anyway? What to watch on television?

Consequently, modern houses don't have a vertical dimension built in. Recreation centers don't need them. Now we all live in single-story, ranch-style houses. Not coincidentally, this fits in with the way we understand the cosmos today. Remember, it has no top. As our cosmologists have told us, we have no fixed points of reference, just empty space.

This is a long way from the cosmos of Abraham and Aeneas. They lived in a *Downton Abbey*–style cosmos with an upper floor. They disagreed about who was upstairs, but they agreed that there was Someone up there. Consequently they built their own households on the same plan.

Without cosmic points of reference by which a father and husband can be said to represent a higher authority, paternal authority, otherwise known as *patriarchy*, is perceived to be the imposition of a father's arbitrary and selfish will. Because few men can bring themselves to actually do this, relationships in households now are based mostly on good feelings.

This is why fatherhood itself has been repurposed. Now dad is a buddy, or a second mommy. (Heather always has two mommies, even when one of them is her father.) The goal of the friendship and nurture is the happiness of the child, as in, "I just want him/her/it to be happy."

This is one more reason why piety itself has been downgraded to a walk in the garden. It is hard to see how duty can apply to the modern family. Duty impresses a structured hierarchy onto our lives. Duty never says, "You be you," or "Go ahead and do what makes you happy." Duty says, "This is who you are; do what is required."

Some people think these developments are all for the better, that old-fashioned households have been replaced by more capacious modern institutions that give us room for more personal freedom. The people who think this way believe Christianity must adapt or die.

But when you adapt you lose something even as you add something. And if you do that often enough, you can become something very different than you were when you began. At what point do you lose yourself, and lose the faith? Perhaps the people that want the faith to adapt actually want the faith to die.

But is adaptation the only option? G.K. Chesterton, the English wit and Christian apologist, once said, "The Christian ideal has not been tried and found wanting. It has been found difficult and left untried."*

What I am going to say next will be hard to hear because it will be hard to put into practice. But I believe that if we try, Christianity can do more than survive. It can thrive, and it can even win.

* From *What's Wrong with the World?*

6

HOUSE STEWARDS

SOMETIMES THINGS GET LOST IN translation; then there are times when they completely disappear. I really do sympathize with translators: translating the Bible is very difficult to do. If you are a translator, my criticisms throughout this book have probably tried your patience. But I actually have family that worked on the New International Version of the Bible. One of them was the chairman of the translating committee. We had long conversations about the challenges of translating the Bible into English. But it was those conversations that helped me to see that translation is a lot more than finding the right word.

For example, what do you do when a word derives its meaning from an institution that no longer exists for the people into whose language you are translating? Do you translate the word with an explanation? And what do you do when you discover that this institution is so significant that the doctrines of creation and even salvation presuppose it? You've got a real problem.

As you have no doubt guessed, the institution I have in mind is the household. And things have been going from bad to worse with that for a while. First, we lost the cosmological basis for the household. Then we lost its economic basis. And now the biological basis is being deconstructed through technology and gender-bending word games. In a world where you can order sperm from a catalog, and it is possible to have three biological parents, can *father* and *mother* or *male* and *female* mean anything normative? That's our brave new world. And because we're losing those points of reference for households, we're losing them for the Church too. And it is starting to show.

Christians have always said that the Church is a house. That's what a temple is, by the way—a house for a god. But just like human households, there's more to them than a physical building. Paul tells us that the real thing when it comes to the Lord's temple is actually God's people working together, like in any economy.*

To oversee the household economy of God you need men appointed for the job. And there is actually a word

* I'm not against church buildings, just like I'm not against physical houses for people. We just need to remember which is the analogy.

for the job in Ephesians—it is οικουμιαν. It appears in Ephesians 1:10 and in 3:2ff. If the word looks familiar to you it is probably because I have referenced the words that make it up repeatedly. It is yet another variation of the Greek words for "house" and "law." Οικουμιαν is the title for the man that serves a house as its steward.

Unfortunately this is not clear in English translations. Those tend to favor words that have acquired their contemporary meanings in corporate bureaucracies. For example, the NASB translates οικουμιαν in Ephesians 1:10 with the word *administration*. (In the ESV you would never know it was there if you didn't look at the Greek.)

But in 3:2 both the NASB and the ESV translate οικουμιαν as *stewardship*. That's better. Stewardship is seldom associated with corporate bureaucracies. But in our time even the word *stewardship* has lost touch with the thing that stewards once cared for. That's why I think translators should make connection explicit by spelling it out; this is why I favor calling these men *house stewards*.

Later in the second chapter of Ephesians, Paul describes the Church as a household (2:19), and then as a temple (2:21). Woven throughout this section of Ephesians is Paul's description of his work as a house steward, but he doesn't see himself as some sort of Lone Ranger. House stewardship is a team effort:

> And he gave the apostles, the prophets, the evangelists, the shepherds and teachers, to equip the saints for the work of ministry, for building up the body of Christ, until we all attain to the unity of the faith and of the knowledge of the Son of God, to mature manhood, to the measure of the stature of the fullness of Christ, so that we may no longer be children, tossed to and fro by the waves and carried about by every wind of doctrine, by human cunning, by craftiness in deceitful schemes. Rather, speaking the truth in love, we are to grow up in every way into him who is the head, into Christ, from whom the whole body, joined and held together by every joint with which it is equipped, when each part is working properly, makes the body grow so that it builds itself up in love. (4:11–16)

As you can see, Paul uses another analogy here. Throughout chapters two to four he toggles back and forth between speaking of the Church as a household and then as a body. And the house and body talk doesn't stop there. It carries forward into chapters five and six, but by then he's not talking about the Church in the same sense, as I hope to show you.

But what does this all have to do with warfare and the cosmos? Paul gives us a glimpse with a significant aside. He tells us that there is an audience for the proclamation of the gospel, which includes the rulers and authorities in the heavenly places (3:10). The gospel reveals the wisdom of God. And that wisdom isn't just a clever aphorism, like something penned by Solomon. It was a stratagem, a bold stroke, as unexpected as lightning from a clear blue sky—Christ rose from the dead and kept on rising. When Christ won His victory, the elect were raised with Him (2:6), and delivered from the misrule of the Prince of the Power of the Air (2:2). Those who were Gentiles in the flesh were made part of the commonwealth of Israel. Where once there had been two peoples living in conflict, now they lived as one people. As the victory of Augustus had brought peace to the Empire, the victory of Christ brought peace to the cosmos, beginning in the Church.

Today, this appears to be the most politically correct thing that we can see in the apostle Paul's ministry. It gives us a biblical basis for racial reconciliation and more. But ironically, it may have been the most controversial in his time. What comes later in chapters five and six was less likely to stir up trouble for him, but in our time it stirs up loads of trouble. What I'm talking about is the household code that he lays out at the end of chapter five and the beginning of chapter six.

I've come across people who believe that the house of God and our houses are only coincidentally related, that the connection in Paul is only a loose analogy. But Paul didn't think that way. For one thing, Paul tells us that one of the qualifications for an elder—a steward in God's house, in other words—is this: he should "manage his own household well" (1 Tim. 3:4). But the connection between the house of God and our houses is deeper than that. For the rest of our time together I intend to show you why.

THE HOUSEHOLD CODES

I never gave the New Testament household codes much thought until I noticed how scrupulously people try to avoid them. That's when I began to suspect that they could be indispensable.

I can't remember ever hearing the codes read aloud in worship, or even discussed in a Bible study. They did come up occasionally when I was studying for the ministry, but only in an off-handed way. I suspect that they embarrass most pastors in the Western world. They are terribly undemocratic, and in the language of our day, they're definitely sexist and classist.

Most contemporary commentators inform us that the codes were a concession to the prejudices of the time. Just why Paul should do this when he could instigate a riot just by showing his face, people don't care to discuss.

THE HERMENEUTIC OF SUSPICION

Biblical scholarship sure isn't what it used to be. At its highest levels it is entirely captive to feminists and their allies. I can recall when they began to assume their chairs at various schools. At first things were not too bad. They had their opinions and you had yours. Now you're not allowed to have yours.

There is a tendentious character to their research. The goal isn't so much to discern the meaning of a text, but instead to uncover hidden agendas. Some have labeled it the *hermeneutic of suspicion*. Hermeneutics is the practice of interpretation. And there are different schools of thought when it comes to how to go about it. The hermeneutic of suspicion assumes the worst about people, especially when it comes to the role of ancient texts in antiquity. Instead of demonstrating that someone in the past was preoccupied with securing his own interests at the expense of others, it assumes he was.

What we have now is character assassination passing as intellectual history. But usually it is done subtly: the sneer, the construal, the aside; these do the trick. And any defense that is proffered by others that is based on the exigencies on the ground is just kicked aside as rationalization.

Some scholars go along with this because they're afraid to lose their jobs. But many scholars are not so pusillanimous: they enjoy pillorying the dead.

Now the hermeneutic of suspicion can be applied to anything, but it is the stuff of daily life that has gotten more than its share of attention. And in particular it is the ancient household that has been pecked to death. And there, the target of all the vitriol, standing like Satan himself, is the *paterfamilias*, the father of the family. Whenever possible, he must be cast in the worst possible light.

One of the ways this is done is by taking things out of their social context. Let's look at an example of what I mean from a book that is better than most. It is Henry O. Maier's *New Testament Christianity in the Roman World*. When addressing the household in antiquity, to his credit he cites Xenophon's *On Household Management*, which was a how-to-do-it manual from the fourth century BC. But it is what he leaves out that misleads his readers.

Here's Maier:

> . . . Xenophon outlines the tasks and duties of a wife. The document takes the form of a dialogue in which Socrates describes how a householder named Ischomachus taught his young teenage wife to manage his estate's household budget, as well as its slaves and domestic production, and even what clothes to set out for him when he went out in public. He also relates how he trained her to control her passions, especially her speech, so as to assure his house was properly regulated and did not bring him public shame.*

Maier sets this in a section dedicated to the oppressive character of women's roles in a household. And the references concerning passions and speech are intended to bring similar statements from the pastoral epistles to mind. But unlike most of Maier's readers, since I've actually read

* Henry O. Maier, *New Testament Christianity in the Roman World* (New York: Oxford University Press, 2018), 151.

Xenophon's dialogue, I know he's left out something important. Based on his treatment of it you wouldn't know that this teenage girl is being trained to take up what would be considered the equivalent of a senior management position in a medium-sized company today. Instead, his tone implies that Ischomachus is muzzling her and that his concern for his reputation is egotistical. Maier doesn't consider the importance of a good reputation to one's livelihood in a small community—a livelihood that this young wife shares, by the way.

This is what happens when you lift social norms out of their social milieu and plop them down in ours. Things get squeezed to fit the categories of our time.

Because I know the dialogue I can assure you that Maier's handling of the text is misleading. Ischomachus actually comes across as a man that many women today would find agreeable. He's commanding, but he is also fair, even tender at times. Here's an example of what I mean. Toward the end of the section in which Ischomachus describes his wife's training he reports saying this to her:

> And the most gratifying thing of all will be is you may turn out to be better than me, and *make me your servant*. This will mean you need not worry that, as the years pass, you will have less standing in the household; *instead you will have more standing in the household*, in proportion to the increase in your value to me as a partner and to our chil-

> dren, as a protector of the home. *For it is virtue rather than physical beauty of youth that increases the true goodness of human life.**

And this is just one of the times Ischomachus departs from the script he's been assigned by feminist ideology.

ANACHRONISTIC THINKING

Another exasperating thing about the hermeneutic of suspicion is the way feminists read back into the past expectations that could only exist in an industrial civilization such as ours. Take the matter of honor culture.

Today the ability to move about without harassment or worse is something most of us take for granted. But in the ancient world safe spaces were very small, usually the insides of households, or tight-knit communities. Standing armies were rare. Rome only managed to form them in the late Republic, and their funding proved to be a very big problem. Police were essentially like the volunteer fire departments in many small towns in America.

For these reasons a woman's physical security depended on the ability of the men in her family or clan to protect her. Forget all that fantasy game nonsense about Xena the Warrior Princess; the story of Dinah in Genesis 34 was the norm.

* Xenophon, *Economics, in Conversations of Socrates*, trans. Robin H. Waterfield (New York: Penguin, 1990), 316; emphasis added.

What does honor have to do with this? Honor bound the members of a household together so that what brought honor to one brought honor to all, and what caused dishonor for one brought the whole family in to disrepute. Just read Jane Austen's *Pride and Prejudice* and you'll see that not too long ago even Anglo-American culture was an honor culture.

Today when we think of honor cultures we tend to think of controlling, even pathological men, and the women they kill for the sake of family honor. We don't think of all the times potential rapists may have said to themselves, "I'll let her alone; I don't want her father and brothers visiting me in the middle of the night."

And this brings me back to my point. We read into the past things that people in the past could not have felt, or even thought, in their wildest fancies.

THE ESCHATOLOGICAL PAUL VERSUS THE COSMOLOGICAL PAUL

When small children want to get their own way, they often set their parents against each other. So long as Mommy and Daddy argue, Junior can do his own thing.

Feminism can be like this. It tends to break up authoritative doctrine so that it can do its own thing. Some feminists have done this by talking about the "Christianities" of early Christianity. What they mean is that back before mean orthodoxy was established, Christianity was a diverse and fluid thing—sort of like Harvard Divinity School—and people could believe all sorts of things about Jesus.

Guess what these people think of the household codes in the New Testament? This is not the Christianity they're looking for. But there are other things in Paul that they do like, Galatians 3:28, for instance, or Paul the Apostle to single people in 1 Corinthians 7. This is a post-familial Paul, a prophet of a heaven-like golden age, the eschaton, that will transvalue all values. But what about the Paul of Colossians, Ephesians, and the pastoral epistles with their household codes and so on? Easy, that's a different Christianity, probably even another guy pretending to be Paul.

You could say that feminists don't like the Paul who talks about the cosmos, or even the Christ that holds all things together. That sounds too Roman, too much like, "Settle down and have a family, you're not going to be a star after all."

Sorry about that slog through the muck of contemporary scholarship, but it was necessary because I suspect you've already heard a mollified version of this in mainstream evangelicalism, particularly in its egalitarian mode.

But the best response to the hermeneutic of suspicion is not a clever riposte. It is sympathy for the dead. We should give the dead their due and try to enter the past imaginatively in order to understand what they had to do to survive in conditions that would be very difficult for most of us to live with.

But even this is not enough. What we really need is a recovery of a way of life. The codes outlined a way to order our households so that they can serve as microcosms of the largest order of them all.

The challenge is enormous. Things are falling apart all around us. The atmosphere of Western culture is poisonous, and it seeps through the cracks and under the doors. It wasn't always so bad. I can even remember when politicians and public intellectuals referred to the family as "the building block of society." What they had in mind had already been so weakened structurally that you couldn't build much with it, but they meant well.

Our households need to recover what made them strong in the past. And to do this you must have a man of the house and a code to guide him so that he can order his house.

Concerning that order, if he is a good steward, his work as a father and a husband will serve as signs of things to come. There are two underappreciated passages in Ephesians that show us how this works. I'll speak to one of them now, and I'll save the other for the next chapter.

EPHESIANS 3:14–15

Paul traces a connection between the cosmos and households in these verses, and he says that it runs through fathers.

Unfortunately, it would be tough to find a better example of "Something was lost in translation" than this passage. Here's how it is rendered in the most literal English translation, the New American Standard Bible (NASB), "For this reason I bow my knees before the Father, from whom every family in heaven and on earth derives its name" (3:14–15).

That last clause makes no sense in English. To understand Paul's meaning you have to read it in Greek. Let me spare you a trip to the bookshelf; here it is in the original: Τούτου χάριν κάμπτω τὰ γόνατά μου πρὸς τὸν πατέρα, ἐξ οὗ πᾶσα πατριὰ ἐν οὐρανοῖς καὶ ἐπὶ γῆς ὀνομάζεται,

Unless you can read Koine Greek, you can't see it there either. But it is as plain as day if you can. His point is etymological in nature; the Greek word that we translate as *family* comes from another Greek word that literally means *father* (πατερα). It is the word πατρια (*patria*). Do you see what this implies? It implies that in the Greek-speaking world of the first century you literally could not say *family* without saying *father*. And Paul says that this says something about the fatherhood of God. The macrocosm is reflected in the microcosm.

Naturally, you shouldn't call yourself a Christian if you can't confess that God created all things visible and invisible. But when it comes to the way most Christians understand the fatherhood of God their thinking is closer to Freud's than to the Apostle Paul's. Like Freud they tend to believe that we project our analogies upwards. (To their credit, they believe someone is actually up there; Freud did not.) But this approach implies that any resemblance between the heavenly Father and human fathers is merely coincidental. There is no real connection. But for Paul, the reason we have fathers—and families as well—is because there is a Father in Heaven. And this, as we will see, makes all the difference in the world.

But what does this mean for a father when it comes to his role in the household? At last it is time to look at the household code in Ephesians.

SLAVERY IN THE HOUSEHOLD CODES

In the household code found in Ephesians the instructions for slaves and masters comes at the end. But I'm going to begin with it before I move on to the rest of the code.

There are three reasons to do this: first, because if you know the code it probably bothers you that Paul didn't emancipate slaves on the spot. Second, because this part of the code tends to be the wedge that progressives use to drive suspicion through every other binding commitment of household piety. We've all heard feminists call marriage slavery, and I can remember the days when curmudgeonly men referred to their wives as their ball and chain. But the third and most important reason for doing so is because in a household slaves and children were alike in one sense, but very different in another. And this is important when it comes to understanding the nature of salvation.

Here is a truth that I would like you to remember: Western civilization did not invent slavery. It can't even claim to have perfected it. The only claim that Western civilization can make when it comes to slavery is that it is the first civilization that figured out a way to live without it.* And we should keep it that way.

With that disclaimer out of the way, just what did Paul have to say to slaves and masters? Here it is, from Ephesians 6:5–9:

> Bondservants, obey your earthly masters with fear and trembling, with a sincere heart, as you would Christ, not by the way of eye-service, as people-pleasers, but as bondservants of Christ, doing the will of God from the heart, rendering service with a good will as to the Lord and not to man, knowing that whatever good anyone does, this he will receive back from the Lord, whether he is a bondservant or is free. Masters, do the same to them, and stop your threatening, knowing that he who is both their Master and yours is in heaven, and that there is no partiality with him.

The way that any institution comes into being and spreads is by solving problems. When it comes to slavery most people understand how it solved the demand problem: people wanted cheap labor and slavery supplied it. It

* See Orlando Patterson, *Freedom in the Making of Western Culture* (New York: Basic Books, 1991).

is the supply side that people miss. It is assumed that people had to be unjustly forced into slavery. But that isn't true.

There were two sources for slaves: debt and displacement. Debt is fairly easy to understand. Sometimes people need things that they can't pay for, so they borrow what they need and promise to pay the debt back later. Later arrives, and they can't pay for one reason or another. What to do? A lender could forgive the debt, that's true. But if he does that, he has effectively paid the debt himself. What if he doesn't want to, or simply can't forgive the debt for one reason or another, what then? If the debtor put up no collateral, then the lender must put the debtor to work.

Today we have the accounting methods and labor-saving devices that make debt slavery more trouble than it is worth. You can just garnish wages or put a lien on a house. But most of the credit should go to innovations in banking. Good loans ameliorate the losses from bad ones, and banks work these losses into their business plans. It isn't a perfect system, but no system is.

Now, returning to displacement, apart from man-stealing—something condemned in the Old Testament, by the way—people could be displaced in a variety of ways: warfare, natural disaster, pestilence, the death of a father, and so on. When these things happened relatives would take you in, ideally. But what if they couldn't, or just wouldn't?

If you're of a more libertarian cast of mind, you may be wondering, "Why didn't people just fend for themselves?"

Well, that's not easy to do when you have no financial resources, no legal status to speak of, and no social welfare beside your extended family. There was wage labor, but that takes liquidity for granted. The liquidity we enjoy today is a recent development. Now, just try to imagine yourself in the shoes of someone who has lost everything. Your choices might be beggary, crime, or being taken into a household as some form of servant, either on a temporary basis, or permanently. Which would you choose?

What I want you to see is that slavery solved a supply problem. And that can be summed up with the question: Where do we put these displaced people?

Still, I've glossed over a lot, and probably new objections have come to mind. But the thing to keep in mind here is that a household was an economy, and everyone worked, even small children. Only the fabulously rich got out of it. All things considered, it is not difficult to see how in the ancient world even the most gentle and generous patriarch could come to find himself the master of slaves almost against his own wishes.

As you can imagine, motivating bond-servants was a challenge. Some masters resorted to force to keep people productive. You can see that Paul addressed the problem of motivation in his code.

But long before Ephesians was written, Xenophon condemned the harsh treatment of slaves. There is actually a lengthy section in his dialogue dedicated to ways bond-servants could be motivated with incentives, even going so far as to give them a share of the profits. Much of his advice sounds like the sort of thing you could read today in a book on business management.

Things work out in unexpected ways. On the great estates, household production became dependent on slave labor. That strengthened demand and led to many abuses. But even in antiquity some thinkers taught that slavery is wrong. And even Aristotle could longingly speculate about a world with robots, and other forms of automation, that would make slavery obsolete.*

In the wide world that the heavenly Father governs, everyone works. Some people work for Him unwillingly, whether they know it or not, because they are slaves to sin. But there are people who have had their debts forgiven. They have been adopted and the Father has made them joint heirs with His only begotten Son (Rom. 8:17).

Speaking of adopted heirs, here is the code as it relates to children, from Ephesians 6:1–4: "Children, obey your parents in the Lord, for this is right. 'Honor your father and mother' (this is the first commandment with a

* "The slave is a possession of the animate sort. [The slave] is an instrument that wields many instruments, for if each of the instruments were able to perform its function on command or by anticipation as they assert those of Daedalus did, or the tripods of Hephaestus (which the poet says 'of their own accord came to the gods' gathering), so that shuttles would weave themselves and picks play the lyre, master craftsmen would no longer have a need for subordinates, or masters for slaves." *Politics*, trans, Carnes Lord (1984; Chicago, IL: University of Chicago, 2013), 6.

promise), 'that it may go well with you and that you may live long in the land'. Fathers, do not provoke your children to anger, but bring them up in the discipline and instruction of the Lord." This is the least controversial portion of the code, but perhaps it would generate more heat if we understood it better. We tend to think of obedience largely within the framework of pedagogy. Children need to obey for their own good; the idea being that obedience will make them good employees. But the code really wasn't intended to help kids to launch, as they say, as though the real world were out there somewhere beyond the household. Households were productive, intergenerational enterprises, and in those days empty nesters were pitied, not congratulated.

In the Ten Commandments the command to honor parents implied the duty to care for them in their old age. This isn't a matter of debate. Commentators as far back as you can go all agree.

Very often the family concerns—the vineyard, the smithy, the boats—were passed on to children with the requisite knowledge for plying the trade, or husbanding the flock, or whatever. And every child hoped to receive a share of an estate. Obviously, that was the premise behind the parable of the prodigal son. So, even though children may have preferred a life of leisure, when they obeyed their parents and worked for them, they were working for themselves in some sense. They had an interest in the property.

It is almost impossible for people to think in this way today. The reason is the vast majority of households in the Western world are proletarian:* they have no property to speak of. Oh sure, someone may have a nice house in a nice neighborhood. But that doesn't count. Dad and Mom usually work for someone else. They sell their time to people that own the businesses they work for.

Today an inheritance is whatever is left in the bank when your parents' assets are liquidated and the bills are paid. Most people do not inherit a farm, or an apartment building, or a business. But in old-fashioned households, property bound the generations together. No wonder honoring parents made for a long life; when you served them you served yourself—and hopefully your children would do the same.

Even if you get my point you may still fail to see how it connects to God's household. Most people don't think of themselves as having a real interest in God's house, and they are not sure what to make of this inheritance that they have been told about. They're used to thinking of their work as earning a reward—like a paycheck, something that can be carried off and enjoyed privately. But that is the way that slaves think, not heirs.

But if we really believe that we have been adopted, and that we are joint heirs with Christ, then what belongs to

* The word *proletarian* was coined by Rome and it meant "free man without property."

us belongs to God, and what belongs to God belongs to us. And working for Him is the same thing as working for ourselves. Galatians 4:1–7 makes this very point about the children of God in His household.

In Paul's time he had a hard time getting his message across because people could hardly believe the good news that they had been adopted. Today people don't know what it really means to be an heir.

This brings me to the last portion of the code, which, if you recall, is actually the beginning. It is the most important part. In the last chapter of this book I will look at the code and its instructions for husbands and wives and all that it implies.

7

THE COSMOS 2.0

PEOPLE ONCE BELIEVED THAT THE COSmos was a crowded place, filled with everything from sprites to archangels—a grand, towering structure reaching up and out of sight. And there we were, in the middle of it all. It was an ennobling place to live.

But today most of us think of the cosmos as empty space. In our minds it has become somewhat like Detroit—a vacant city, crumbling all around. The old gods are long gone, and even Christians have a hard time believing in angels. And when it comes to Jesus, He lives with us inwardly, in the garden of the heart.

When the light of Christ's glory appeared, it revealed that there was really nothing to the old gods. But His glory also filled the empty spaces, and the Church moved in and grew. Christians cleaned house, but even so they hung pictures of the old gods on the walls, thinking that just because they had never existed it didn't mean that they didn't have something to say. Christianity was a capacious and vibrant place in those days, a cathedral filled with seemingly contradictory things. And beneath its soaring heights new things were built, things that had never been seen before: universities and hospitals, as well as the greatest civilization the world has ever known.

Heaven had not come to earth; that civilization had its faults, its sins—but on the scale of relative goods, it was the best there ever was.

But it was destroyed by a new way of seeing. No, the invention of the telescope didn't destroy that civilization. Atheism should get the blame for undermining it—atheism, that way of seeing that doesn't see. Atheists tell us that there is no intrinsic meaning to things because there is no God to give them meaning. Some atheists were urbane and cagey, like David Hume, others were violent and tyrannical, like Vladimir Lenin, and yet others were just pulp-fiction popularizers, like H.G. Wells and H.P. Lovecraft. But they all agreed: In the end the cosmos amounts to nothing.

At first fools rose in applause. "There's nothing above; at last we can rise!" But wiser fools knew that no Heaven means no "up." Everything is moving but going nowhere. Outer space swallows everything but is never full. Now we have philosophers that say things like, "A boy is a pig, and a pig is a boy." And consciousness itself offends our brightest lights. Here's Bertrand Russell in 1903: "I have been merely oppressed by the weariness and tedium and vanity of things lately: nothing stirs me, nothing seems worth doing or worth having done: the only thing that I strongly *feel* worth while would be to murder as many people as possible so as to diminish the amount of consciousness in the world. These things have to be lived through: there is nothing to do about them."*

And that was *before* two world wars.

First we lost the gods, then we lost the one true God, and now we're losing ourselves. We're dying.

When people believe in the future, they tend to fill it with little copies of themselves. Children are a vote of confidence. Today, the most pampered people in the history of the world can't be bothered. Some of them go so far as to say that having children would be immoral—a crime against the planet, or something like that. Meanwhile they grow ever more dependent upon the poor immigrants that mow their lawns, and fix their plumbing, and someday will sponge-bathe them in their gated retirement communities.

The empty cosmos of the atheists has left us empty. But empty places don't stay empty for long. The cosmos

* Letter to Gilbert Murray, dated March, 1903 in Russell's Autobiography (1998; London: Routledge, 1971), 167.

is being repopulated. Jesus told a little story along this line in Matthew 12:43–45.

> "When the unclean spirit has gone out of a person, it passes through waterless places seeking rest, but finds none. Then it says, 'I will return to my house from which I came.' And when it comes, it finds the house empty, swept, and put in order. Then it goes and brings with it seven other spirits more evil than itself, and they enter and dwell there, and the last state of that person is worse than the first. So also will it be with this evil generation."

The last state is worst than the first. Can you see it? The monsters are coming.

What becomes of people when they turn away from the light? They deform. Things lose proportion; little things swell grotesquely, while other things that were meant to be large and vigorous, shrivel. At least the old pagans had things to focus their minds upon; today we stare into the void.

The twentieth century was full of hollow men whose emptiness filled the world with dead. There were Stalin, Hitler, and Mao, and those monsters had many little helpers. But they also had larger masters, because human beings are not the only form of intelligent life in the cosmos. There are also principalities and powers, those fallen angels that we are doubly blind to, not just because they are invisible, but because we don't acknowledge their existence.

KEEP CALM AND CARRY ON

One of the things that conservatives should conserve is the belief that history has a Governor. As awful as things can be, someone is ordering things to their given ends. Even the age that we live in serves a purpose in the great scheme of things.

This means that we are the true progressives. We know that things are going somewhere good. Guerrilla piety serves that good, and it fights for it. From here on out I'll try my best to show you what it all adds up to.

WHAT'S THE POINT?

What does one say to a civilization that is lost in the cosmos? I think my dowsing rods can help: There's one more place where the stories of Aeneas and Abraham cross—both are supposed to end with a marriage.

Aeneas waged a war for a princess. Only when his woman was won would he be able to take his throne and reign with her. But his story ends before that can happen. Instead of a happy ending with a king and queen seated next to each other, we're left with moral ambiguity when Aeneas kills his rival. That's because it was at this point in the telling of the story that Virgil died, and the story ends. So the *Aeneid* ends on a down note, because Virgil's death made certain that the story ends with a death and not a new beginning.

But Abraham's story ends on a high note. In a marvelous paradox, Abraham is long dead by then. But someone else who's died becomes very much alive. Another war was waged by a hero for a princess, and once she was won, she became a queen, but not of a little kingdom in the center of Italy. She became queen of the Cosmos. And the Bible ends with their wedding day. And they live happily ever after that. Here's the coronation of the queen from Revelation 19:6–8 and 21:1–4:

> Then I heard what seemed to be the voice of a great multitude, like the roar of many waters and like the sound of mighty peals of thunder, crying out,
>
> "Hallelujah!
> For the Lord our God
> the Almighty reigns.
> Let us rejoice and exult
> and give him the glory,
> for the marriage supper of the Lamb has come,
> and his Bride has made herself ready;
> it was granted her to clothe herself
> with fine linen, bright and pure"—
>
> for the fine linen is the righteous deeds of the saints.
>
> Then I saw a new heaven and a new earth, for the first heaven and the first earth had passed away, and the sea was no more. And I saw the holy city, new Jerusalem, coming down out of heaven from God, prepared as a bride adorned for her husband. And I heard a loud voice from the throne say-

> ing, "Behold, the dwelling place of God is with man. He will dwell with them, and they will be his people, and God himself will be with them as their God. He will wipe away every tear from their eyes, and death shall be no more, neither shall there be mourning, nor crying, nor pain anymore, for the former things have passed away."

The cosmos has a future. There will be a new Heaven and a new earth. Elements of the original cosmos will carry over, and that is really good news because the redeemed are included in what gets carried over.

We live by the light of tomorrow's sun, and that sun is the Lord God (Rev. 22:5). This is the basis of our piety, the substance of our daily duties.

ONE FINAL OBJECTION: NO MARRIAGE IN THE RESURRECTION

Isn't it odd that some Christians believe that marriage is a second-rate institution? Even though this teaching was soundly condemned by the Reformers it is experiencing something of a revival among their urban children in places like New York City and San Francisco.

A favorite proof-text for these people is Matthew 22:30, "For in the resurrection they neither marry nor are given in marriage, but are like angels in heaven." A surface reading might lead you to believe that Jesus endorses a post-familial faith. But wait, there's more to it.

Recall, the case in point was actually a debate between Jesus and the Sadducees over the resurrection. The Sadducees used Mosaic law concerning the pious duty of a brother to care for his brother's widow in order to tie Jesus up in a knot of logic. Here's the trap they set: a woman runs through seven brothers, each dying after he has married the widow. This leads to the stumper, "Whose wife is she in the resurrection?" They thought that they had Jesus in a Gordian knot—but their major premise was faulty. And Jesus just cuts the cord with one stroke—"there is no marriage in the resurrection."

People who use this to downgrade marriage forget a larger point made elsewhere. Marriage doesn't actually come to an end at the resurrection.

If you're married, I'm not talking about your marriage. That marriage will come to an end. But the end of your marriage is not the end of marriage. On the contrary, marriage will grow so large it will fill the cosmos and fundamentally change it. Allow me to explain.

HUSBANDS AND WIVES

At last I'm ready to look at the most controversial part of the household code. It contains a profound mystery. And that mystery is our window to the world of tomorrow. Yet it is deeply offensive to many of the people who say they can't wait for the world to come.

Here it is, Ephesians 5:22–33:

> Wives, submit to your own husbands, as to the Lord. For the husband is the head of the wife even as Christ is the head of the church, his body, and is himself its Savior. Now as the church submits to Christ, so also wives should submit in everything to their husbands.
>
> Husbands, love your wives, as Christ loved the church and gave herself up for her, that he might sanctify her, having cleansed her by the washing of water with the word, so that he might present the church to himself in splendor, without spot or wrinkle or any such thing, that she might be holy and without blemish. In the same way husbands should love their wives as their own bodies. He who loves his wife loves himself. For no one ever hated his own flesh, but nourishes and cherishes it, just as Christ does the church, because we are members of his body. "Therefore a man shall leave his father and mother and hold fast to his wife, and the two shall become one flesh." This mystery is profound, and I am saying that it refers to Christ and the church. However, let each of you love his wife as himself, and let the wife see that she respects her husband.

There have been many objections raised to the arrangement over the years, some of them having to do with the trustworthiness or competence of a particular husband. But is it the husband, or is submission the real problem? Let's test it. Try to picture the best husband imaginable. Would it really make a difference? Some women say it would be different being married to Jesus. Paul anticipates this and says, okay, use your husband as a stand-in for Jesus. Does it help? Probably not.

Let's admit it, submission can be very disagreeable no matter who the man is; even when he is the image of the invisible God.

But submission is required. It is always required. Every human institution in the history of the world has been held together by it. We tend to mollify this awkward fact by using more palatable terms, like *compliance*. This is intended to keep authority figures out of sight. But authorities are still working behind the scenes in even the most liberal and light-filled bureaucracy.

Nevertheless it is easy to justify obstinacy. Sometimes a boss really is an idiot; sometimes a police officer really is brutal; sometimes a politician really is corrupt—and sometimes rebellion really is the only solution. But you can't build anything on rebellion. Submission will eventually be called for: armies can't win without submission, and football teams can't score without submission, and children can't learn math without submission, and businesses can't make a profit without submission. We can be honest about it, or we can try to hide it—this is life. And it is true for the house of God, and for the households we live in. And Paul makes the connection: "For the husband is the head of the wife even as Christ is the head of the church."

Understood in the right way, submission is something to be proud of. Just think of the command *Attack!* and the valor we admire when men rise in obedience to charge. And this brings up the real problem people have with the household codes: they don't believe that the sacrifices that they call for are worth making. They don't believe that households serve a higher purpose than the personal goals of the individuals that live in them.

When preachers read the code aloud, they tend to move on quickly from submission to "husbands love your wives." But that is as much a command as the command for wives to obey their husbands. It fails to register controversy for some reason, although it should, because the reason Paul gives for men to love their wives is that a wife is a man's own body. Perhaps the reason this fails to offend is the fog that tends to fill our minds whenever the word love is mentioned.

For, if a wife is a man's body, then she belongs to him in some sense. This was something taken as a matter of course not too long ago. While Paul doesn't say it here, it is also true that a husband's body belongs to his wife. And he does say that very thing elsewhere (1 Cor. 7:1–4). Today all of this is contested because people believe that they belong only to themselves. They think their bodies are inviolable and impregnable things, bound to other people only by a thin cord of consent. But if this is so, then our unions are only as strong as our will—and that even goes for our union with Christ.

But salvation depends upon something stronger than a human will, because no human will, no matter how strong, can raise the dead. The Christian hope is not based on consent, but on belonging to God. Our bodies belong to Him. We are not our own.

THE BODY OF CHRIST

If you're familiar with the rest of Paul's work, this ought to bring to mind another passage in which he refers to a body. There he calls the Church the body of Christ (1 Cor. 12:12–31).

Just so you know, Paul didn't invent this way of talking. The history of philosophy is full of references to communities as bodies. And when the idiom is used, there is always a head attached. It is apropos because even though heads and bodies can be identified as distinct things, they form a single purposeful thing, just like a community when it is working well. And here in Ephesians Paul calls this single, purposeful thing "one flesh." The implication of this is quite startling for husbands and wives. It means that a household is a little community. And on the flip side, the communion of Christ and the Church is a marriage.

Now, allow me to raise something for your consideration that may be the furthest thing from your mind right now. I'd like you to consider the doctrine of *double imputation*.

DOUBLE-IMPUTATION AND ONE FLESH

You may not be familiar with the word "imputation," but it isn't hard to understand. Essentially it refers to a transfer of either a credit or a debt from one person to another. For example, if you were to co-sign a loan, if the person you co-sign for defaults on the loan, the debt is imputed to you—you have to pay it. So basically "imputation" is an accounting term.

Christians from other theological traditions sometimes chide the Reformed Christians for being a sect of accountants. We're precise, we're cerebral, and we like starched shirts and pocket protectors. But salvation really is accounting.

Most Christians are familiar with salvation as accounting, but they think in terms of single-imputation. They believe that our sins have been imputed to Christ and that's why He died on the cross, so that He could pay for them. But that's where it stops for them. They think that Christ's death has left them with a zero balance.

But we all know that salvation is more than having your debts cleared. It also includes getting credit for something that we didn't do. Here's what I mean: when Christ rose from the dead the Church rose with Him. None of us deserve that, only Christ does. But we receive what He deserves because His righteousness is imputed to us. So there are two imputations here. Christ gets what we deserve, and we get what Christ deserves. And this is where marriage comes in.

Marriage is one of the most beautiful things in the world, and it is consummated when a man and a woman become one flesh. Paul tells us it is a mystery, meaning that it hides something, even as it reveals something.

But a conjugal union is just the beginning; one flesh also refers to the natural issue of that union in children. And it goes even beyond that: it is a union of interests, of goods, a common life, and a common future. It means that what goes for one, goes for the other. And Paul tells us that *all of this* applies to Christ and the Church. What belongs to the Church, belongs to Christ; and what belongs to Christ, belongs to the Church, because they are *one flesh*.

Hopefully you can now see how marriage and double imputation overlap. Because sinners are condemned to die, Christ died for His chosen bride—that's the first imputation; but here's the other—because Christ was raised and glorified, the Church is raised and glorified, too. That's the second imputation.

I hope you see what this implies when it comes to Christian piety.

MARRIAGE IS THE END OF THE WORLD

It means that, in a real way, conjugal marriage is the end of the world. It connects this world to the next, it unites Heaven and earth, and it is a sign that reads, "This is the way the world will end, not with a bang, not with a whimper, but with wedding bells."

EPILOGUE: GUERRILLA PIETY MADE PLAIN

"HIS DISCIPLES SAID, 'AH, NOW YOU ARE speaking plainly and not using figurative speech!'" (John 16:29).

Whether people understand them or not, figures of speech are often the only way to get a message across that will survive the generations. This is because they often draw on things that are universal in nature, and not bound by time or place. And that's why they can help us to see, even when we don't fully understand what we're looking at.

That's what the word *theory* means, by the way. It comes from the Greek θεορος, for spectator. It is also where we get the English word *theater*. Good theories help us to see reality. When people move on to practice without seeing, they can't understand how their actions fit into a larger picture. But if there is a figure of speech, at least their practice can possibly grow into an understanding. It would be great if the order was always figure of speech, understanding, then doing; but often it is figure of speech, doing, then understanding. And sometimes understanding never comes. (Sometimes doing never comes!)

I'm reminded of the complaint I hear all the time about philosophers—that they're ivory-tower theorists. Usually the complainant lives in the shadows cast by philosophers that died about two hundred years ago. What passes for common sense to him was once a radical philosophy.

In this book I've tried to help you see something. It isn't something that I've dreamed up. The image is found in the Bible and it is the revelation of the future of the cosmos. But paradoxically we can actually fit our lives into it if we see the big picture.

GUERRILLA PIETY

In this book I've tried to show you that we live in a cosmos that is at war with itself. And like Aeneas, Christians have been given suits of armor and they are duty-bound to fight for the household of God. But like Christians in the first century we are hopelessly overmatched on the ground. The principalities continue to rage against the Lord of the Cosmos. Their inhuman machinery menaces us, particularly in the West. The state continues to grow and centralize, technology tracks us (and increasingly it is used to manipulate us), progressive multinational corporations standardize us and commodify us, popular media seek to indoctrinate us and addict us, and state-run education and healthcare are eliminating private rivals so as to make us ever more dependent on government largess. All of these things and more are arrayed against us.

In spite of all of these things, Christ has already won. He is our Lord and we are engaged in a long obedience. We wrestle with His enemies.

Our way or war was described by Paul in Ephesians. In fact, my conviction has grown over time that this epistle is a handbook of guerrilla piety. In it Paul outlines a two-pronged strategy to follow.

STRATAGEM 1: THE HOUSEHOLD OF GOD

When Alexander the Great swept across the East, he left behind a trail of seventy cities bearing his name—Alexandria—and one named for his horse. It was more than an ego trip; they served a purpose. Naturally, Paul knew all about them. And the greatest of them is still an important city today—Alexandria, Egypt.

Those cities helped to promote the Greek way of life in the regions of his conquest. They were model communities, gifts of "the divine Alexander," intended to help enlighten his new subjects.

The churches Paul planted throughout the Roman world performed the same function. And in those houses of God, the house stewards worked to make sure that these communities put the benefits of Christ's rule on display for the principalities and powers.

Of course, the benefits enjoyed by the members of these churches are good in themselves. Word and sacrament serve as a stairway to Heaven, as well as a virtual time machine. When believers worship they rise to heavenly places where they are seated with the risen Lord. They are also sent into the past to sit at the feet of the prophets and the apostles, and they are also flung into the future, where by faith they dimly discern, as though a glass, a day when all things will be done on earth as they are in Heaven.

It is important to keep these things in mind, because when we turn the Church into the watergirl for a secular culture in the name of "relevance," the Church loses touch with the standard that guides her work. There is something of a paradox here: When the Church chases the world, she loses herself; but when the Church chases Heaven, she gains the world.

STRATAGEM 2: THE HOUSEHOLD, FULCRUM OF THE COSMOS

We have the fulcrum of the world in our possession, and that gives us leverage. I am talking about our households. But the principalities know this, and that is why they are obsessively working to break them down.

You may wonder how your small stake could possibly threaten the powers that be. Just remember, a household ordered by the household code in Ephesians reflects the rule of Christ. Besides that, all things connect. That little tune that your household sings is in harmony with the music of the spheres, and that harmony restores many things that the enemy has perverted.

The reason households have leverage is that they are natural. The household codes perfect its intrinsic structure by ordering it to its true purpose in Christ. The principalities lack genuinely creative power, so they depend on households to bring people into the world. And when the machinery of the state arrogates this task to itself, invariably it produces damaged goods. So human authorities tend to vacillate between undermining households and supporting them. It largely depends on whether or not a culture's gatekeepers recognize their true interests in them at any given time. Very often they cannot. Those are particularly bad times. But whenever the spring of renewal is in the air, things can change suddenly.

When it comes to the practical matter of establishing a productive household, I have written about it in detail elsewhere.* When I finished that book, I could see even then that I would need to write this one. The previous book is more of a nuts-and-bolts book, and this one is intended to show readers how a household fits into the really big picture of the cosmos and the world to come. But there is one thing from that earlier book that I must add before I conclude this one.

Households have been the basis of human culture from the start. When Eve was given to Adam, the seed sower was given another garden—its fair to say that she was a garden within the garden—and the work of human cultivation began. It was the most natural thing in the world, we're talking about having children, after all. But the fruitfulness of the first household didn't end there. There was another garden to tend to. And there still is. Every household should hold something that husbands and wives can tend together so that they can be fruitful in every way. What they tend should be theirs, otherwise they work for someone else.

If the things they tend are fruitful, they can live on them. And if these things belong to them, they enjoy a measure of independence they could not enjoy otherwise. I mentioned examples of this earlier: a farm, a trade, a small business, even intellectual property. I like to lump

* *Man of the House* (Eugene, OR: Wipf and Stock, 2017).

examples of this sort of thing under the label *productive property*.

People used to understand how important productive property is when it comes to the health and independence of households. In fact, when the United States won its independence, roughly 80% or more of households in the new nation owned the means of their livelihood—we were a nation of proprietors. Today it is closer to 10%. We have become a nation of wage earners. Consequently we're more likely to be influenced by "the culture," especially by the schemes of liberal elites in media, academia, and government. For households to recover their culture-making influence there must be a large-scale revival of proprietorship, and that means bringing productive property back home where it belongs.

There is a lot more that could be said, but you shouldn't expect me to say it all. I have my blind spots, and even things that I have said could have been said more profoundly by someone else. Hopefully as the recovery of the productive household will gain momentum, more and more people will want to write about it.

So fight the good fight. Go home, build a house, and if you do it in the right way, you will give the world a glimpse of things to come. There is nothing more terrifying to the principalities than this. Because in the end, the principalities will bow and confess the Lordship of Christ, and if your house is ordered well, it is a reminder of that glorious day (Phil. 2:10–11). And, as hard as it is to imagine, when, at the end of the war for the cosmos, the tribunal for war-crimes is impaneled, you and I will have our seats behind the bench (1 Cor. 6:3).